T0170478

Kwame Nkrumah

OHIO SHORT HISTORIES OF AFRICA

This series of Ohio Short Histories of Africa is meant for those who are looking for a brief but lively introduction to a wide range of topics in African history, politics, and biography, written by some of the leading experts in their fields.

Kwame Nkrumah

Visions of Liberation

Jeffrey S. Ahlman

OHIO UNIVERSITY PRESS
ATHENS

Ohio University Press, Athens, Ohio 45701
ohioswallow.com
© 2021 by Ohio University Press
All rights reserved

Printed in the United States of America
Ohio University Press books are printed on acid-free paper ∞ ™

31 30 29 28 27 26 25 24 23 22 21 5 4 3 2 1

Library of Congress Cataloging-in-Publication Data

Names: Ahlman, Jeffrey S., 1982– author.
Title: Kwame Nkrumah : visions of liberation / Jeffrey S. Ahlman.
Other titles: Ohio short histories of Africa.
Description: Athens : Ohio University Press, 2021. | Series: Ohio
short histories of Africa | Includes bibliographical references and
index.
Identifiers: LCCN 2020048193 (print) | LCCN 2020048194 (ebook) |
ISBN 9780821424520 (paperback) | ISBN 9780821447390 (pdf)
Subjects: LCSH: Nkrumah, Kwame, 1909–1972. |
Presidents—Ghana—Biography. | Pan-Africanism—History—20th
century. | Ghana—Politics and government—1957–1979.
Classification: LCC DT512.3.N57 A66 2021 (print) | LCC
DT512.3.N57 (ebook) | DDC 966.7051092—dc23
LC record available at https://lccn.loc.gov/2020048193
LC ebook record available at https://lccn.loc.gov/2020048194

Contents

Illustrations

Map

Figures

Acknowledgments

In 2017, following the launch of my first book on Nkrumah-era Ghana, *Living with Nkrumahism: Nation, State, and Pan-Africanism in Ghana,* Gillian Berchowitz asked me if I would be interested in writing a biography of Kwame Nkrumah for the Ohio Short Histories of Africa series. I initially wavered. Approximately six months later, she contacted me again about writing the biography. It was through her persistence and foresight that this project came about. Following Gill's retirement, Ricky Huard, Stephanie Williams, and Sally Welch, among many others at Ohio University Press, helped shepherd the project to completion in the midst of a global pandemic. I cannot thank them enough for their patience and assistance.

The project is based upon approximately seventeen years of research on Nkrumah-era Ghana. My debts in Ghana, the United States, and beyond are too many to list in these short acknowledgments. However, they include those who talked to me about their experiences in 1950s and 1960s Ghana; archivists, teachers, and friends who introduced me to new archival collections and lines of thought; colleagues who have read numerous drafts of articles, chapters, and other materials on Nkrumah and life in midcentury Ghana; institutions that funded my research, most recently including the National Endowment for the Humanities and Smith College; my family who endured writing times; and students who have helped me think more deeply about decolonization, pan-Africanism, and the politics of both hope and disappointment that surround any discussion of Nkrumah and Africa's path to independence. This book could not have been written without you all.

Abbreviations

AAPC	All-African People's Conference
ADM	Administrative Files
BAA	Bureau of African Affairs
CIAS	Conference of Independent African States
CPP	Convention People's Party
CYO	Committee on Youth Organisations
GCR	Gold Coast Regiment
GPRL	George Padmore Research Library on African Affairs
IAFE	International African Friends of Ethiopia
MP	Member of Parliament
NCBWA	National Congress of British West Africa
NLC	National Liberation Council
PAF	Pan-African Federation
PRAAD	Public Records and Archives Administration Department
RG	Record Group
RLAA	Research Library on African Affairs
UGCC	United Gold Coast Convention
UNIA	Universal Negro Improvement Association
UP	United Party
VRP	Volta River Project
WASU	West African Student Union
WANS	West African National Secretariat

Kwame Nkrumah

A Transnational Life

Few individuals exemplify the richness and depth of the world that shaped twentieth-century Africa more than Kwame Nkrumah. At its foundation, Nkrumah's biography necessarily subverts both the intentional and unintentional constraints of what have emerged in both popular and scholarly works as two-dimensional representations of the African past. Like many of his generation, Nkrumah lived a life that spanned multiple historical and historiographical worlds. As a child and young man, Nkrumah came of age in the emerging imperial world of the early Gold Coast (colonial Ghana). Attending a Catholic primary school in the far southwestern Gold Coast town of Half Assini before gaining admission into one of the first matriculating classes at the new Achimota Secondary School just outside the Gold Coast capital of Accra, Nkrumah's early years were fundamentally marked by both the visible and the invisible changes ushered into Gold Coast life by the onset of formal colonial rule. After Achimota, Nkrumah—through the help of the Nigerian nationalist and Accra-based newspaper editor Nnamdi Azikiwe—traveled to the United States to attend Lincoln University, a historically Black college in rural Pennsylvania. Spending approximately a decade in the United States, Nkrumah witnessed American life at the height of the Great Depression and the Second World War. Even more importantly, he confronted life and politics as a Black man in Jim Crow–era America.

In May 1945, Nkrumah again shifted historical contexts, leaving the United States just as the European war was ending. Following his arrival in London, Nkrumah committed himself to the city's Black anticolonial circles, where, working alongside the Trinidadian pan-Africanist George Padmore, he helped organize the 1945 Manchester Pan-African Congress. Famed for its call for an immediate end to European colonial rule in Africa and the Caribbean, the Manchester Congress at once resurrected a pan-African movement that—at least in its most prominent manifestations—had arguably been dormant since the 1920s, while also creating a political environment for African anticolonial nationalists like Nkrumah to explore their shared experiences, struggles, and ambitions for the continent.

Nkrumah's 1947 return to the Gold Coast ushered in another new era in his life, during which he would organize one of Africa's first mass political parties. In doing so, he and his fellow party organizers drew women, workers, ex-servicemen, farmers, and youth, among others, to a political movement that was national in scope and was founded upon the expressed goal of "Self-Government Now." In 1951, in the Gold Coast's first popularly contested elections, it was these diverse groups of people who would catapult Nkrumah into his first political office as the so-called leader of government business. A year later his title was elevated to that of prime minister, a position cemented by large general-election victories in 1954 and 1956. In office, Nkrumah and his government ultimately oversaw the Gold Coast's transition to self-rule and the 1957 creation of an independent Ghana, which would become an inspiration throughout Africa and its diaspora. Moreover, in the new Ghana, Nkrumah quickly embraced the enthusiasm created by the country's independence, transforming pan-African manifestations of Ghana's independence into a fundamental and, for some in Ghana, controversial part of the new Ghanaian identity he sought to inculcate in the populace.

Nkrumah's presidency infamously came to an end in February 1966 as portions of the Ghanaian military and police overthrew him and his Convention People's Party (CPP) government while he traveled abroad. Following the coup, Nkrumah went into exile in the Guinean capital of Conakry. At the invitation of Guinea's first president, Sékou Touré, Nkrumah accepted the ceremonial title of co-president in Guinea—a title created to honor both Nkrumah's role in advancing the pan-African cause on the continent during his tenure in office in Ghana and Nkrumah's role in helping stabilize Guinea after that country's abrupt independence in 1958. However, the experience of the coup further radicalized the former Ghanaian leader as he now began to more actively argue for the legitimacy of anticolonial violence and guerilla warfare in Africa's continued fight against neocolonial exploitation in all its forms. It was this political vision that Nkrumah carried to his death in 1972.

* * *

Debates and discussions of Nkrumah and his legacy, however, rarely center on Nkrumah alone. Rather, they have long been interwoven into Ghanaian, continental, and diasporic reflections on Ghana's and Africa's past and future. In December 1999, for instance, debates surrounding Nkrumah rose to the forefront of the Ghanaian and African political stage as the BBC World Service conducted a continent-wide poll in which the news agency asked its African listeners to vote for the continent's "Man of the Millennium." More than thirty years after his 1966 overthrow and a little more than a quarter century after his 1972 death, Kwame Nkrumah beat out the individual who many might have assumed would be the favorite for the honor, Nelson Mandela.[1] The historical context in which this poll took place is particularly important. Initially undertaken to commemorate the new millennium, the vote came at a

Map 1.1. Map of Ghana, ca. 1960. Produced by the Smith College Spatial Analysis Lab.

time when much of the world remained riveted by the recent liberation of South Africa and, particularly in the West, the idea of the "Rainbow Nation" put forward by Mandela and Desmond Tutu. Moreover, just months earlier Mandela had added to his international acclaim as he did what few African politicians had done before him—leave office voluntarily after one term. Yet for the BBC's African listeners, Nkrumah and his legacy in both Ghana and Africa not only resonated with them more but, more importantly, also represented something different from that offered by the much-respected Mandela. For them, Nkrumah and the visions he had articulated for both Ghana and Africa in the 1950s and 1960s at once represented the still remaining vestiges of the hope and aspirations of the bygone era of African independence and—marked by his overthrow—the disappointments of that era's demise.

The BBC's poll results did not go unnoticed within Ghana itself. In January 2000, for instance, columnist Kwame Nsiah took issue with the vote in the *Ghanaian Chronicle*. To this end, he rejected the renewed triumphalist narrative developing around Nkrumah implicit in the BBC poll result, arguing that Nkrumah's foremost contribution to Ghana and Africa was that he "paved the way to Africa's corrupt politics of our time." According to Nsiah, "His [Nkrumah's] politics successfully destroyed almost every institution of democracy, making politics a scare for many and dirty for all."[2] Over the course of the next decade and beyond, key commentators in the Ghanaian press and blogosphere have consistently returned to the poll in their discussions of Nkrumah and Ghanaian politics more broadly, contentiously renewing often vitriolic debates over Nkrumah's complicated and even divisive legacy in the country. In doing so, these figures have integrated this seemingly simple listener poll into a longstanding process of discursive innovation in Ghana around the life, legacy, and even body of Nkrumah. At the heart of this process is thus the continuous construction and reconstruction of the image of Nkrumah—Nkrumah-as-liberator, Nkrumah-as-authoritarian, Nkrumah-as-Ghanaian, and Nkrumah-as-pan-Africanist, among others—and the integration of these images into broader debates over the state and fate of the Ghanaian nation.

The challenge for those interested in the life and legacy of Kwame Nkrumah is that, in part through the contestations over his legacy, Nkrumah has come to represent an enigma. As the BBC poll and the reaction to it illustrate, Nkrumah means many things to many different people. Moreover, what he means and to whom has changed over time and continues to change. In the 1950s and 1960s he was simultaneously viewed across Africa and significant parts of the African Diaspora as a—if not *the*—hero of African liberation and, for many in some countries, as a threat to their national autonomy as their governments accused Nkrumah and the government he led of meddling in their internal affairs. Even Mandela complained in his diary that the pan-African anticolonial machine that Nkrumah had made famous in Ghana had "turned out to be something quite contrary to what it was meant to be."[3] Others, meanwhile, insisted that it was with Nkrumah and his vision of a liberated and united Africa that Africa's and the global Black community's future rested.[4] In Ghana, as Nsiah's response to the BBC poll indicates, similar debates occurred, for Ghanaians who lived through the heady days of the 1950s and the 1960s regularly balance stories of an ambitious, imaginative, and innovative leader with tales of an Nkrumah-led government that generated wide-ranging fears of political detention throughout the populace.[5]

In the decades since the 1966 coup that overthrew Nkrumah and especially his 1972 death, debates surrounding the memory and legacy of Nkrumah in Ghana and Africa alike have not waned, as the debates unleashed by the BBC poll indicate. Over the years, Nkrumah has come to represent everything from hope, joy, and African self-determination and dignity, in a global context where such things cannot be taken for granted, to, as Nsiah suggests, corruption and decline. Moreover, in contrast to the debates over Nkrumah that preceded these more contemporary reflections, posthumous debates surrounding the Ghanaian politician were only rarely about Nkrumah himself. Instead, Nkrumah—his life, experiences, and career—served as a mechanism for Ghanaians, Africans, and others to make sense of their changing relationships to and anxieties with the continuously evolving postcolonial nation and state. Across the continent, the 1970s and 1980s in particular was a period of precarity in which not only had the dreams of the independence era given way to despair in much of the continent, but, just as importantly and with a few notable exceptions, the continent appeared to have lost its dreamers. Those who remained, like Thomas Sankara, in neighboring Burkina Faso, often suffered fates worse than Nkrumah.[6] In Ghana specifically, the period was foremost one of political and economic disarray marked by coups, food shortages, and uncertainty. More than just nostalgia for a past lost, the memory and image of Nkrumah thus often became a stand-in for more complex and deeper reflections on an alternative future robbed of the continent by inept and extractive politicians, neocolonial powers abroad, and, for some, the perceived apathy of their fellow Africans writ large.

By the 1990s and early 2000s, as Ghana and much of the continent ostensibly transitioned into multiparty democracies, Nkrumah again rose within the public and popular imagination. At the center of these reflections on Nkrumah were the promise and disappointments of the post–Cold War world. For many outside Africa, particularly within journalistic and certain academic circles, the end of the Cold War represented a victory for freedom and democracy as the Soviet Union and its brand of communism dissolved, purportedly transforming the Soviet Union and its various satellite states into fledgling capitalist democracies. In Africa, the euphoria of the post–Cold War world found its most visible expression in a wave of democratic constitutional reforms in the last decade of the twentieth century. Between 1989 and 2003, for instance, all but four of sub-Saharan Africa's forty-eight states would, at a minimum, hold de jure contested elections.[7] Ghana itself held a referendum on a new constitution in early 1992, with the country holding its first multiparty elections in over a decade later that year. However, as elections took place throughout Africa, what could not be broken was the political elite's hold on power as, throughout much of the continent, including Ghana, the political elite responded more to the free-market fetishization of the global order than the spoken and unspoken social contracts linking it to the populace over which it governed. As a result, by the early 2000s Ghanaians, Africans, leftists, and others would regularly come to marshal Nkrumah and his political project as a response to the calcifying inequality of Africa's neoliberal age. Nkrumah, his pan-Africanism, and especially his focus on African economic self-determination stood as a shadow narrative to the claims of a "rising Africa"—mostly tied to the continent's perceived openness for business—coming from the halls of the continent's ruling parties, the World Bank, the International Monetary Fund, the United Nations, and the West more broadly.

For scholars and others interested in Nkrumah himself, midcentury Ghana, or twentieth-century Africa, the wide-ranging ways in which Nkrumah and his legacy have been deployed over the past sixty-plus years have provided many challenges. In histories of midcentury Ghana, for instance, scholars have found it difficult to disentangle perception from reality and myth from memory in their histories. In my own previous research on Nkrumah-era Ghana, popular reflections on Nkrumah almost necessarily deviated toward normative questions over whether Nkrumah was "good" or "bad" for Ghana or if he succeeded or failed, with many also extending these Ghanaian debates to the continental level.[8] In Ghana, as suggested, the Manichean nature of these discussions belies the much deeper contemporary and historical undertones driving the debates. However, in the decades since Nkrumah's overthrow scholars have tended to replicate variations of these debates in their own work on Nkrumah, often judging him by an imaginary social-scientific scorecard tied to their own expectations for the postcolonial Ghana that Nkrumah led. In perhaps the most famous example of such a form of scholarly assessment, the prominent Kenyan political scientist Ali Mazrui declared in 1966 that through Nkrumah's role in leading the Gold Coast to its 1957 independence and subsequently his commitment to continental unity, "Nkrumah was a great Gold Coaster" and a "great African." However, through what Mazrui saw as the "excesses" of Nkrumah's leadership in Ghana, "Nkrumah fell short of becoming a great Ghanaian."[9]

As my previous work on Nkrumah-era Ghana has argued, the shortcomings of such an approach to understanding early postcolonial politics and life in Africa are many. At the forefront of these challenges is the question of historicization, for, as scholars, journalists, and other commentators default to these normative assessments of African politics, they tend to strip from the African political and social context its specificity. In doing so, they make impossible sustained and nuanced analyses of not only specific African historical contexts, but, just as importantly, explorations into the ways in which those contexts have changed due to the actions and reactions of a diverse array of historical actors to different local and global stimuli. In Ghana specifically, the relative dearth of archival sources on the Nkrumah era, coupled with the well-documented biases of the colonial record, have in many ways further buttressed such an approach to the twentieth-century African past, feeding both into and from the more popular public narratives surrounding Nkrumah, his life, and legacy. The result has often been a set of flattened pictures of Nkrumah, Gold Coast/Ghanaian politics, and the transnational political, social, and cultural networks that came to shape them as well as twentieth-century Africa more broadly.

* * *

This biography thus has multiple aims. As with all biographies, it strives to provide a clear understanding of the richness and depth of its subject's life and experiences as well as an appreciation of the complexity of the subject's memory and legacy. The breadth of Nkrumah's experiences fundamentally requires a historical lens capable of focusing on the specificities of Nkrumah's life and choices and one that zooms out to position Nkrumah as part of a rotating array of interrelated historical contexts. For academic historians in particular, such a perspective has proved particularly challenging as they have largely operated in a historical discipline that has, for all intents and purposes, divided itself along temporal and geographical lines. For those interested in figures like Nkrumah, then, not only have they had to grapple with the many historical contexts that comprised the lives of Nkrumah and many of his contemporaries, but they have also been forced to confront the distinct historiographical traditions and perspectives of those varying contexts—historiographies that only rarely speak to one another directly.

As discussed earlier, at the popular level, the varied nature of Nkrumah's experiences inside and outside of Ghana has helped to create the context in which diverse groups of peoples have had the opportunity to construct their own sets of "Nkrumahs." The overarching narrative surrounding these varied "Nkrumahs" may lead them to bear similarities to one another. Many, for instance, rely on the popular trope in African history of the "big man," tying Nkrumah and his legacy to what could be read as highly masculinist interpretations of what Ghana and/or Africa could be or could have been.

Moreover, Nkrumah himself often traded in such masculinist personal and national imagery in a variety of venues, including in his 1957 autobiography.[10] Others, including the CPP and those opposed to Nkrumah and his party, would at various times also turn to such narrative construction. However, in building these narratives, different features of Nkrumah's life, choices, and experiences tend to be stressed. Even more importantly, the political and moral lessons one is to take from Nkrumah's biography not only shift with the unique political, social, and cultural concerns of the ones reconstructing Nkrumah's life story, but also with the changing historical circumstances. Rather, like the narrative of the Ghanaian nation more broadly, the narrative of Nkrumah's life in the Ghanaian, African, and global popular imagination is a moving target that itself requires its own historicization and contextualization.

At the center of any biography of Nkrumah, then, is the question of how to bring the various images of Nkrumah into dialogue with one another. The task, however, is not one of mere acknowledgment or narration. It is also not one limited to Nkrumah himself. In both life and legacy, Nkrumah is a figure that embodies the rapidly changing, if not chaotic, nature of the long twentieth century. In the Gold Coast/Ghana, like much of Africa, the first decades of the twentieth century marked the maturation of the modern colonial project, while the middle decades represented its demise and the final decades the growing disillusionment with both the legacies of decolonization and the African status quo. However, as Nkrumah himself in the first three-quarters of the century and his memory after that encountered these changing historical moments, new forms of networks (regional, national, imperial, and transnational) were created to sustain themselves. For Nkrumah in his life, such network building was foremost embodied in the continuously growing list of peoples, institutions, and ideas he strove to bring into his orbit. As I have previously argued in regard to his political philosophy, "Nkrumahism," the eclectic nature of the ideas that came together to compose his political and social thought makes it difficult to properly define Nkrumahism with much precision, particularly in a philosophical sense. Moreover, Nkrumahism also meant different things to different people, and what it meant even to Nkrumah changed in important ways over time.[11]

This eclecticism was a feature of Nkrumah's life as well. Even more importantly, it is in this diversity and, in some cases, also in the internal tensions and contradictions that that diversity brought on that make Nkrumah's life and worldview so politically and intellectually rewarding. Perhaps more than any other figure in twentieth-century Africa, he and his philosophy embodied a politics of bricolage: a politics that sought to bring people together by building and experimenting with new forms of political, social, cultural, and economic connection. As noted, for some a sense of excitement and hope pervaded Nkrumah's political, social, and cultural experimentation. Looking to him personally, some saw in him a cosmopolitanism that, in Ghana, promised to transform the country into the epicenter of the new Africa, while in Africa and in the diaspora he opened spaces for new imaginings of an envisioned global Black community that would claim a powerful and equal voice on the international stage. Others, disillusioned by the often draconian methods Nkrumah and his government employed in their attempts to make their vision a reality, feared what could be lost in this transition, and as they opposed Nkrumah's policies, many also increasingly feared for their own safety.

To this end, the goals of this biography do differ from that of a simple narration of Nkrumah's life story. In addition to the more traditional biographical structure, this book views Nkrumah's life story itself as an arena of contestation that must be historicized in dialogue with the more conventional biographical narrative. To many in Ghana specifically, the hopes, dreams, anxieties, and fears aroused by the Nkrumah era and Nkrumah himself did not disappear with Nkrumah's 1966 ouster—or even his death. Rather, for many, they are very much still alive, articulating themselves in nuanced and often hidden and unexpected ways in the many intertwined historical contexts—colonial, imperial, national, continental, and transnational—that have come together to comprise Ghanaian life and politics.

In other words, Nkrumah has an equally important afterlife that is intimately interwoven throughout both popular and scholarly understandings of his more classical biography. Thus, I contend that such a reframing of Nkrumah's life story in this biography refocuses the historical narrative by presenting Nkrumah as both the subject of the biography and as a lens into asking broader questions surrounding the political and social changes marking twentieth-century Africa. What arises, then, through a reflection on Ghanaians', Africans', and others' invocations of Nkrumah is a recognition of the process of negotiation between past and present that continuously drives Ghanaians' and others' wide-ranging debates over the "nation" in its many different meanings.

As a result, in addition to this introductory chapter, six additional chapters comprise this biography. The book's second chapter traces Nkrumah's childhood and young adulthood in the Gold Coast. Born in the far-western Gold Coast town of Nkroful, Nkrumah came of age in a period in the Gold Coast in which the formal colonial stage was coalescing. Transitioning from its late-nineteenth-century creation into a more professionalized governmental administration, the colonial state of Nkrumah's youth was at once becoming increasingly bureaucratic and, despite its rhetoric of indirect rule, expanding its reach—wittingly and unwittingly—into new aspects of Gold Coast life. As a result of this transition, as the chapter discusses, it helped catalyze a shift in how wide segments of the Gold Coast populace understood the political and social world around them and the opportunities that world could afford. For Nkrumah and his family, like many others, education became key in this new world, for education had the potential of opening new networks of opportunity and engagement—intellectual, professional, and political—for those lucky enough to go to school and particularly for the select few, like Nkrumah, who made it to the colony's premier secondary schools.

The book's third chapter details Nkrumah's experiences in the United States and Great Britain. Comprising more than a decade of his life (1935–47), this period marked not only his self-described political awakening, but, just as importantly, the broadening of his worldview as he explored and experimented with a range of political philosophies and activist networks that at times even transcended both diasporic and continental politics. As a number of scholars have shown, it was during this time that Nkrumah's political and social thought began to take shape and mature. However, this chapter goes beyond such an appraisal by emphasizing the changing diasporic and global political contexts that marked Nkrumah's time abroad and his emerging politics. These included the Depression-era and wartime United States, American racial politics, and the anticolonial and pan-African politics of the postwar United Kingdom.

The book's fourth and fifth chapters interrogate Nkrumah's 1947 return to the Gold Coast and his rise on the Gold Coast/Ghanaian political scene. These chapters distinguish themselves from the largely chronological framework of other biographies of Nkrumah's tenure on the Gold Coast/Ghanaian political stage, most of which constrain themselves to the detailing of Nkrumah's elevation from an anticolonial agitator to prime minister and finally, in 1960, to president. In contrast, the chapters emphasize the broader tension in Nkrumah's politics and thought as he sought to balance the structural constraints of territorially defined nationalist mobilization with his own and others' pan-African ambitions for Ghana, the continent, and the global Black community. In doing so, the chapters highlight the wide-ranging era of political experimentation that marked Nkrumah's time in office. Not only was this a time for defining the political and social parameters of the new Ghanaian nation, but it was also one of redefining Africa in the emerging international community.

The book's sixth chapter examines Nkrumah's life in exile following the 1966 coup that overthrew him. The general perception of this time in Nkrumah's life was one of an exiled ex-president plotting fruitlessly to make his return to Ghana as part of a countercoup. Nkrumah did spend much of his time making such plans. However, as the chapter details, this period was also a time in which Nkrumah actively began to rethink his postcolonial vision for Ghana and Africa, further radicalizing himself and his political philosophy as he confronted a continental and global political reality that, to his mind, had fully succumbed to the dangers of neocolonialism. As a result, the development of his political philosophy in exile reflects a much more sustained engagement with ideas of anti-imperial violence, guerilla warfare, and class struggle in the politics and praxis of African liberation.

The book's final chapter provides the space for continuing reflections on the many conflicting legacies of Nkrumah as a thinker, anticolonial activist, and political leader in Ghana, Africa, and the African Diaspora. The chapter opens with the reactions to Nkrumah's 1972 death and the controversies surrounding who had rights to his body—his exiled home of Guinea, the town of Nkroful, or the Ghanaian state—thus setting the stage for many of the subsequent contestations over his legacy that have marked his postmortem history. As this biography as a whole illustrates, Nkrumah is a figure who has been resurrected many times in the nearly four decades since his death. For many Ghanaians living in the aftermath of decolonization's disappointments, structural adjustment's dismantling of the infrastructure of the postcolonial state, and the ever-widening inequalities of neoliberal multiparty democracy, the prospect of an Nkrumah now among the ancestors continues to embed itself in deep-seated battles over the future of the Ghanaian nation. Meanwhile, continentally and in the diaspora, Nkrumah at once continues to represent the hope of a shared pan-African future and the constraints to that future created by the continuing power of global capitalism and imperialism.

2

Empire and a Colonial Youth

In March 1957, Kwame Nkrumah stood on a stage in the Old Polo Grounds in Accra, the capital of the colonial Gold Coast, and ushered in the birth of the new Ghana. Over much of the previous decade, Nkrumah and the Convention People's Party (CPP) he had founded had agitated against the British for a path to self-governance. Following the Gold Coast's 1951 elections that culminated in Nkrumah's release from prison and elevation to the role of leader of government business and later prime minister (see chapter 4), Nkrumah formed his own government in the Gold Coast, negotiating with the British and further pressuring them from the inside for what would become Ghana's 1957 independence. Additional electoral victories in 1954 and 1956 further solidified Nkrumah's and the CPP's position at the center of the Gold Coast political stage, yet masked an array of tensions within the colony as to the meaning and nature of the nation under construction. In the central forests of the contemporary Ashanti Region, for instance, groups of cocoa farmers—eventually joined by key figures in the Asante state and even some prominent members of Nkrumah's CPP—challenged Nkrumah and the CPP's vision of a unitary postcolonial Ghanaian nation with a nationalism of their own centered on the distinctiveness of the Asante past. Other religious and ethnic groups in the colony would also come to argue for recognition of their own distinct nations within the broader emerging Ghanaian nation. Through 1955 and the first half of 1956, violence followed these debates in parts of the Gold Coast. Even following the CPP's final preindependence election victory in mid-1956 and Britain's announcement of a date for Ghanaian independence, threats of Asante secession tempered the celebrations surrounding the preparations for Ghana's independence.[1]

However, as Nkrumah began to speak at midnight on March 6, 1957, the thousands below him in the crowd cheered not just the end of colonial rule in the new country and a perceived conclusion to the tumult that had marked the Gold Coast politics of the previous six years. Perhaps even more importantly, they began the process of imagining what their future would look like going forward. Onstage, Nkrumah, along with several other prominent officials from the CPP, came to embody this process of imagination. Moreover, Nkrumah himself—donning one of the CPP's famed "PG" (Prison Graduate) caps of Gandhian inspiration and adorned in a smock popular in the new country's northernmost regions so as to signify the CPP's connections to all parts

Figure 2.1. Kwame Nkrumah's speech on Ghana's independence, March 6, 1957. Photo by Mark Kauffman from the LIFE Picture Collection. Reproduced courtesy of Getty Images.

of the new Ghana—did not wait to have the vision for Ghana's future defined by others. Instead, as he spoke, he insisted that with Ghana's independence he, the CPP, and the Ghanaian public writ large were not done fighting. As a result, in what by far has become his most famous declaration, Nkrumah pronounced to the audience before him that Ghana's "independence is meaningless unless it is linked up with the total liberation of the African continent."[2]

At the heart of Nkrumah's independence-day pronouncement was a political project aimed at the construction of a new Ghana, a new Africa, and, most expansively, a new world. This was to be not only a world in which Ghanaians and Africans alike would be accepted on their own terms, but, even more importantly, a world that they would also have an active voice in forging. However, it was also a project of destruction, for it was to be a project tied to the destruction of the world that colonialism had built. It was a project that, while building something new, also aimed to tear down the racism, inequality, and exploitation that, in the new Ghanaian prime minister's eyes, were fundamental to the colonial project in Africa and beyond. In 1963, writing in the midst of the continental debates that would result in the formation of the Organization of African Unity, Nkrumah sought to remind those in both Ghana and Africa of the stakes of this reinvention. In doing so, he emphasized that the ravages of colonialism were sown deep in African society and were often manifested in peoples' lives in unexpected ways. "The social effects of colonialism," Nkrumah explained in *Africa Must Unite,* "are more insidious than the political and economic. This is because they go deep into the minds of the people and therefore take longer to eradicate. The Europeans relegated us to the position of inferiors in every aspect of our everyday life." Moreover, he emphasized, "Many of our people came to accept the view that we were an inferior people. It was only when the validity of that concept was questioned that the stirrings of revolt began and the whole structure of colonial rule came under attack."[3]

The world that Nkrumah envisioned Africa's decolonization as deconstructing was also one that was inescapable and that had helped forge him into the individual, politician, and political thinker he had become.[4]

As a region, the Gold Coast (colonial Ghana) had a long history of interactions with Europeans dating back to the fifteenth century with the arrival of the Portuguese along the Gulf of Guinea. Attracted to the region's gold trade, an array of additional European powers followed suit over the next two centuries, including the Dutch, British, Danish, Swedish, and Brandenburgers, among others. As the French merchant and slaver Jean Barbot described at the end of the seventeenth century, the "Gold Coast, which the Portuguese call 'Costa d'Oro' and the Dutch 'Goudt-kust,' derives its name from the metal which is found in great abundance in its mines and among the sands of its river."[5] By the second half of the seventeenth century, however, European interest in the Gold Coast gradually shifted away from the region's gold supply to the trade in people. As a result, over the course of the seventeenth century, just under a hundred thousand individuals would be sold into slavery and transported across the Atlantic as part of the transatlantic slave trade.[6] The next century witnessed an even more drastic growth of the slave trade from the Gold Coast, with more than one million individuals becoming subject to the horrors of the trade and the Middle Passage.[7]

By the time of Nkrumah's officially accepted birth year, 1909, the legal, external slave trade in the Gold Coast had been abolished for a century, although an illegal trade from the Gold Coast would continue through the 1830s. For Gold Coasters, abolition marked the beginning of a period of political and economic transformation and uncertainty that would persist for more than a hundred years, thus shaping the experiences of Nkrumah's entire generation of Gold Coasters. At the forefront of this transformation was the rise of a new cash-crop economy throughout much of the region, especially in the southern third of what now forms the contemporary Ghanaian state. Through much of the mid- to late nineteenth century, this trade centered on the region's oil palm industry, particularly in the sale of palm oil and palm kernels. In Europe, manufacturers turned to these products for use in everything from soap to industrial lubrication to the production of nitroglycerin needed for dynamite. By the time of Nkrumah's birth, however, the oil palm industry had given way to the new crop of cocoa, catapulting the Gold Coast into one of the world's leading producers of the crop by the beginning of the First World War. As numerous scholars have emphasized, cocoa's rapid rise sent shockwaves throughout the region, transforming the ways in which Gold Coasters understood land, money, family, marriage, social mobility, and parenting, among many other key features of Gold Coast life.

As the Gold Coast's cash-crop revolution took off in the nineteenth and early twentieth centuries, Gold Coasters also witnessed a political landscape that was fundamentally in flux. In the region's central forests, for instance, the Asante state—the most powerful state in the region—found itself in the nineteenth century in a nearly century-long period of political turmoil. In many ways, as the Asante state sought to adjust to the region's new economic realities and an encroaching European presence on its borders, which included a series of wars with the British, the nineteenth century fundamentally tested the cohesion of the famed empire. By the last quarter of the century, Asante was in a state of civil war. It would ultimately fall to the British in 1901. Meanwhile, beginning in the mid-nineteenth century, the British in particular began to exert ever more influence in the Gold Coast's political affairs, embarking upon a gradual process of political and economic infiltration that would culminate in the 1874 creation of the Gold Coast colonial state. As elsewhere on the continent, the actual extension of colonial rule into people's lives did not necessarily coincide with the declared establishment of the colonial state. Rather, it entailed a more than three-decade-long process of coercion, violence, and negotiation for the colonial state to take shape.

A similar process of transition was occurring in Nkrumah's native Nzema in the far southwestern Gold Coast in the decades surrounding Nkrumah's birth. Known to the Europeans who visited the Gulf of Guinea coast as the kingdom of Appolonia, the Nzema state had emerged as a strong centralized power by the end of the eighteenth century. Its growth mirrored the process of state-building that marked many of the Gold Coast's other new Akan states in the seventeenth and eighteenth centuries. By the mid-nineteenth century, however, increasing political and economic intrusion into Nzema affairs from European merchants and officials had weakened the state, culminating in a civil war of its own following Britain's midcentury arrest of the Nzema king, Kaku Aka. The result was a division of Nzemaland into eastern and western districts, with Nkrumah's birthplace of Nkroful in the east. Through the final decades of the nineteenth century, disputes between the two Nzema groups would feature prominently in the region's local politics as chiefs and rulers from both Eastern and Western Nzema—officially known as Eastern and Western Appolonia until 1924—made claims seeking to reunite the Nzema under single rule again. At the same time, the Nzema, like others throughout the Gold Coast, also witnessed the continuously growing influence of the British on their daily political, economic, and social lives during the final decades of the nineteenth century and the first years of the twentieth.

* * *

In the 1950s and 1960s, Kwame Nkrumah viewed the increasing presence and infiltration of colonial rule into Gold Coast life as the root of the political and social upheaval of the nineteenth and early twentieth centuries. Yet it was also this rapidly changing political and social landscape in Nzemaland and beyond that would shape Nkrumah's youth and the choices open to him. For those interested in Nkrumah, though, his early life has proven particularly difficult to historicize, for—like most Gold Coasters of the era—the historical record surrounding him and his family is nearly nonexistent. From what is available, most importantly via his 1957 autobiography (a text that, despite its shortcomings, guides any historian's understanding of Nkrumah's first decades), it can be assumed that Nkrumah's childhood and youth were similar to those of most Gold Coasters in the early twentieth century in that, in the moment of rapid transformation occurring in the still relatively young colony, he, as a child, most likely would not have recognized the extent of the changes brought on by the encroaching colonial state, particularly in terms of how he viewed his daily life.

The effects of Gold Coast colonialism on his and most Gold Coasters' daily lives were subtle. As Nkrumah suggested in his autobiography, his childhood was far removed from the direct trauma of colonial rule. Rather, he contended that he had a happy childhood surrounded by an active and caring family and community. As with most Akan, which includes the Nzema, Nkrumah's family followed a matrilineal line of descent. In practice, this meant that Nkrumah belonged to his mother's family (*abusua*). Nkrumah, however, would only spend his first three years in Nkroful before traveling by foot west with his mother to the town of Half Assini to join his father. As Nkrumah would recall more than four decades later, the journey of approximately seventy-five kilometers took three days. Upon arriving in Half Assini, Nkrumah—his mother's only child—joined an extended family that included several siblings born of his father's other wives, along with his siblings' mothers. The compound in which they all lived, Nkrumah reminisced, was marked by constant activity, always full and bustling with women, children, and visitors. As for Nkrumah, he described himself as a child as "probably one of the most willful and naughtiest of [his father's] children." Despite his rambunctious nature, Nkrumah remained extremely close to his mother, to the point that he often insisted on sleeping alongside her even during his father's visits to their home—much to his father's annoyance.[8]

As Nkrumah aged, the question of schooling arose. In his autobiography, Nkrumah presented his enrollment in a local Catholic primary school as due to the ambition of his mother, who, he emphasized, had not had the opportunity to go to school herself.[9] Nkrumah's portrayal of his family's decision to send him to school overshadows, however, his own relative exceptionality in gaining access to a formal education in the Gold Coast during the first decades of the twentieth century. At the most basic level, Western-style schools had been present in the Gold Coast since the early sixteenth century, with the Portuguese constructing the first school in the region in the central coastal town of Elmina in 1529. The Dutch would establish their first schools approximately a century later, followed by the British. In all these schools, the curriculum was heavily imbued with Christian messages. In each case, though, they only served a minute segment of the Gold Coast population and almost never anyone from the Gold Coast's interior. Instead, through at least the eighteenth century, the most notable, but not exclusive, constituencies for the Gold Coast's schools were the children born of the relationships of European merchants and African women.[10]

By the nineteenth century educational opportunities in the Gold Coast would expand exponentially. Over the first half of the century, many of the opportunities were in schools founded by the region's various merchant companies. By midcentury, the merchants would largely fade from the Gold Coast educational landscape as missionary influence in the region intensified. Along the coast, the Wesleyans would establish at least twenty day schools by 1850, while further east in Accra and Akuapem the Basel Mission established its own boarding schools. The British administration also maintained a select number of its own schools. However, in 1850, the administration only had one such school on record, a school in Cape Coast Castle. By the end of the century it would still only record seven such schools in the Gold Coast, educating approximately seventeen hundred boys and girls. At the same time, mission schools educated nearly eleven thousand students.[11] Despite the growth in the number of schools and students, though, the more than twelve thousand students in Gold Coast schools at the turn of the century still only represented less than 1 percent of the 1.3 million people in the Gold Coast at the time.[12]

Further west in Nzemaland, educational opportunities were even more scarce than in the historically more cosmopolitan areas surrounding Cape Coast and Accra. Moreover, for families, sending even a single child to school often required substantial sacrifices as many struggled to pay the requisite school fees to gain admittance to a particular school. Even more challenging for many was the consistent maintenance of the fees required to keep a child in school through the primary level, let alone beyond. As a result, school fees emerged as a constant source of conflict in many Gold Coast families as mothers, fathers, and members of the child's broader family negotiated responsibility for a child's fees. School fees—in part connected to schooling's relative newness, preexisting norms connected to fatherly obligations, and the fees' sheer constancy—"cut right to the heart of daily negotiations over childrearing," as two prominent scholars of Ghana have explained. Over the course of the early twentieth century, responsibility for these fees would gradually fall on fathers and, even more fundamentally, would come to symbolize what it meant to be a good father in the Gold Coast and Ghana.[13] These scholars were writing on early twentieth-century Asante, yet their observations are applicable to much of the southern Gold Coast more broadly. In the case of Nkrumah's education specifically, his family's negotiations over school fees appeared to follow this trajectory, with his father taking up much of the financial burden of his education despite Nkrumah's own reflections that his schooling was largely his mother's passion project. Moreover, Nkrumah himself also personally contributed to his educational costs by raising and selling chickens, which, according to him, allowed him to fund the additional costs associated with schooling, such as the purchase of books.[14]

Despite the financial strain schooling placed upon not only Nkrumah's family but families throughout the early twentieth-century Gold Coast, an increasing number of Gold Coasters—like Nkrumah's mother in particular—viewed a child's education as the key to the future. For them, the cost associated with a child's schooling was at its foundation an investment in social mobility. For the colony's established educated elite, however, such a utilitarian vision of education proved frustrating. Writing in 1907, for instance, in the nationalist newspaper the *Gold Coast Leader,* the newspaper's editors chided parents and students for what they presented as Gold Coast families' narrow and self-interested views connecting education to ladder climbing. "The 'Bread-and-butter' object [in schooling] . . . is an impelling motive . . . [and] not altogether undesirable," the newspaper proclaimed. However, such a motive was also self-defeating in that it failed to cultivate within an individual the values, skills, and know-how needed for the "best service to humanity." As a result, the newspaper declared that "larger-life education aims at the development of the highest type of manhood and womanhood for the best social efficacy."[15] More broadly, the editors of the *Gold Coast Leader*—along with those of many of the Gold Coast's other nationalist, African-run newspapers—understood the creation of an educated population not as a personal or even familial good. Rather, they viewed it as a collective project, one central to their key objective of modernizing the Gold Coast—politically, socially, and culturally—and positioning the colony on a path toward eventual self-governance.

In most Gold Coast families, however, such high-minded arguments likely fell on deaf ears. Instead, Gold Coasters came to understand education as a key feature of their adaptation to the rapidly changing social and economic context of the colonial era. Most notably, Gold Coast families viewed it as providing an opening for their children to enter into an array of wage-earning occupations, including in the Gold Coast civil service, teaching, bookkeeping, and serving as clerks in a variety of different middle-class, white-collar businesses. For an economy increasingly reliant on a cash-based system of exchange, such wage employment proved key to an individual's and family's social and material advancement. It helped provide them with the means to do everything from sending more children to school to buying land so that they might try their hand at joining the region's various new cash-crop industries, including cocoa, rubber, and copra, to name a few. Others built houses, invested in lorries, and used their employment to help make them more eligible marriage partners. To this end, as was the case with Nkrumah, most of the schoolchildren of his generation did not come from the colony's established families, such as those who ran newspapers like the *Gold Coast Leader*—a class of barristers, ministers, businessmen, and others—or from the colony's traditional elite. Rather, they largely represented a social class consisting of farmers, traders, and artisans aiming to secure a better life for themselves and their families within the confines of the new political, social, and economic realities associated with the burgeoning colonial state.

However, at many Gold Coast schools in the early twentieth century, key parts of the curriculum were not directly designed to promote a sense of social mobility in the schools' students. Instead, the curriculum of most colonial-era schools aimed to serve the administrative and ideological interests of the various European institutions established in British West Africa. In the case of most mission schools, like the one Nkrumah attended, curricula regularly combined traditional academic coursework in literacy and mathematics with religious, vocational, and agricultural training. As far back as at least the mid-nineteenth century, missionaries and others interested in Africa had presented such an integrated curriculum as foundational to what they understood as Africans' social and spiritual advancement. In 1840, for instance, the British abolitionist Thomas Fowell Buxton, writing to an audience purportedly interested in eradicating the remaining elements of the slave trade in Africa, presented education, Christianity, and labor on the land as the pillars of slavery's abolition. As outlined by

Buxton, this triad would open the continent to "legitimate commerce." Furthermore, he claimed that "civilization will advance as the natural effect, and Christianity operate as the proximate cause of this happy change."[16] Aspects of Buxton's ideas carried their way into the Gold Coast as a variety of different mission schools sought to inculcate the colony's schoolchildren in the values, mores, and ideals of what, as defined by the missions, it meant to be a modern or "civilized" man or woman in the world.[17] Nkrumah's primary school curriculum almost certainly followed a similar model and mission.

For many students, Nkrumah included, such a project was at least initially an alienating one. In the case of Nkrumah specifically, he claimed that he maintained an initial dislike of the rigor and discipline of the school's curriculum. In contrast to his earlier childhood, where he basked in a freedom that allowed him to play, eat, and socialize with little adult intervention, the classroom required not only timeliness and attendance but an obedience that was enforced with corporal punishment.[18] Nkrumah was not alone in needing time to adjust to the rigors of the school day. In conversations with historian Stephan Miescher, for instance, one woman who attended school during approximately the same period—albeit several hundred kilometers north in contemporary Ghana's Ahafo Region—emphasized that both boys and girls endured the threat of the cane at school, leading her parents to confront the teacher. The teacher retaliated by subsequently ignoring the student in class. Likewise, other individuals also emphasized how the school uniform, the freedom from many household responsibilities, and expectations of church attendance distinguished and, in some cases, distanced them socially from other children their age who did not attend school.[19]

Despite his initial frustrations, however, Nkrumah claimed that he eventually came to embrace the classroom and the opportunities opened to him as well as the limitations it placed on his life. In particular, Nkrumah explained in his autobiography how his schooling in Half Assini had encouraged him to take an active role in the church. According to him, this passion for the church was cultivated by a German priest named George Fischer who, in Nkrumah's words, came to "take a liking to me" and pushed the young Nkrumah in his education. Nkrumah recalled that Fischer "became almost my guardian during my early school days and"—most importantly—"so relieved my parents of most of the responsibility with regard to my primary education." By extension, during this time Nkrumah would regularly take part in Mass and, with the support of his recently baptized mother and Fischer, would be baptized into the Roman Catholic Church.[20]

* * *

Following the completion of his primary school education, Nkrumah took over his own classroom in Half

Assini, serving for one year in his late teenage years as a pupil-teacher. However, in 1926, an official from Accra's Governmental Training College visited Nkrumah's classroom and invited him to enroll as a student in the training college. Shortly after Nkrumah's arrival, the colonial government merged the training college with the new school it was opening just outside of Accra in Achimota. Formally inaugurated in 1927 as the Prince of Wales Training College and School, the Achimota School, as it later came to be known, represented the colonial government's most ambitious attempt at translating the proclaimed ideals of indirect rule into a new model of "Africanized" education during the 1920s and 1930s. Aimed at nurturing a student into young adulthood, the Achimota curriculum envisioned a system of total education—spiritual, social, cultural, political, and moral—that was to produce a new population of educated Africans with the moral and social authority necessary for the merging of the principles and values of Africa's past with the skills and standards of an imperially defined modern world. As Gold Coast governor Gordon Guggisberg explained in 1919, "Our aim [in education] must be not to denationalise them [the people of the Gold Coast], but to graft skillfully on to their national characteristics the best attributes of modern civilisation. For without preserving his national characteristics and his sympathy and touch with the great illiterate masses of his own people," Guggisberg continued, "no man can ever become a leader in progress, whatever other sort of leader he may become."[21]

The educational ambitions Guggisberg held for Achimota were not unique in interwar British imperial circles. Rather, they tended to reflect the racial and paternalist assumptions that undergirded the stated aims of the colonial project itself. In his 1938 *African Survey,* for instance, a nearly two-thousand-page report aimed at rethinking British colonial policy on the continent, Lord Malcolm Hailey—who in the early 1920s had served as the governor of Punjab in British India—insisted that few subjects were as highly contested in Africa and among colonial officials as the nature of African education. As he argued: "The problem of native education [in Africa] is peculiar because the circumstances of an undeveloped race are fundamentally different from those of a homogenous and relatively static modern community. In such a community, the chief function of education is to maintain the continuity of culture by transmitting to successive generations not only accumulated knowledge but acquired standards of value and conduct; in Africa education is, and is intended to be, an instrument of change." Achimota, for him, was thus envisioned to be a model of this change as, in his words, the institution was aimed at "the production of a type of student who is Western in his intellectual attitude towards life, but who remains African in sympathy."[22]

More broadly, the philosophical and pedagogical underpinnings of Achimota were part of a wider rethinking of the colonial project in the Gold Coast and in Africa as a whole in the interwar years, particularly in terms of the role of the colonial administration in African life. Accompanying the school's founding in 1927, for instance, were equally prominent investments in the colony's infrastructure. Most notably, these investments included the construction of Takoradi harbor in the western Gold Coast, which was to serve as the colony's first industrial harbor, and Korle Bu Hospital in Accra—the colony's first teaching hospital. Moreover, the 1920s also marked a rapid extension of the colony's railway and road networks and the Gold Coast's further integration into postwar international trade networks. As viewed by Guggisberg, the decade of the 1920s was to be one of sustained modernization and progress. To this end, the newly appointed governor promised the Gold Coast Legislative Council that, in what he perceived to be his stewardship of the Gold Coast, he would "always be guided by the fact that I am an Engineer, sent out here to superintend the construction of a broad Highway of Progress along which the races of the Gold Coast may advance, by gentle gradients over the Ridges of Difficulty and by easy curves around the Swamps of Doubt and Superstition, to those far-off Cities of Promise—the Cities of Final Development, Wealth and Happiness."[23]

In addition to these infrastructural projects, Guggisberg also advanced a new Gold Coast constitution, implemented in 1926. At the heart of the new constitution was the introduction of a slightly more democratic structure to the colony's governance, providing for a reconstituted Legislative Council and a network of

Provincial Councils of Chiefs based in each of the colony's three provinces.[24] Not dissimilar to his pronouncements regarding his infrastructural ambitions for the colony, Guggisberg viewed his administration's role in the Gold Coast with the new constitution as theoretically laying the groundwork for a possible path to eventual African self-governance. Albeit, Guggisberg and others in the Gold Coast administration understood this eventual path to self-governance as occurring in some undefined time in the future and to be shepherded on British terms. In the meantime, the Gold Coast Legislative Council and the colonial administration, it was argued, were to work together to create what Guggisberg and his colleagues viewed as a political culture in the colony that was to be tied at once to modern, liberal traditions and to what they understood as the distinctiveness of the Gold Coast national identity.[25]

The investments made by the Guggisberg government in the 1920s Gold Coast ushered in a period of increased governmental intervention in Gold Coast life and institutions, which was in many ways exemplified by the Achimota curriculum. Key to the Achimota curriculum was the idea that African students were at their core works-in-progress who had to be both nurtured and pushed. Not dissimilar to the mission schools that predated Achimota, general coursework in language arts, mathematics, and the social sciences comprised the core of the school's educational program. These academic subjects, however, were also to be combined with a strong focus on vocational training, manual labor, religion, and—largely distinct from many of the school's predecessors—African culture, namely in its performative dimensions. For one of the school's founders and its most prominent African faculty member, J. E. K. Aggrey—who Nkrumah would regularly cite as one of his idols—such a curriculum promised to educate and, in turn, transform the whole individual into the modern ideal. "With the coming of Western civilization," Aggrey—in many ways echoing Guggisberg and Hailey—explained to a 1926 wireless audience in Great Britain and Ireland, "African boys and girls tended to cut loose from tribal ties. In many instances the educated became neither Western nor African, losing the best in both and often imbibing the worst of both." Achimota, by contrast, was not only envisioned as a means by which to restore an emphasis on the uniqueness of Gold Coast culture in the student body, but, in doing so, also promised to reconnect students to the land and soil itself. As a result, Aggrey emphasized that the Achimota curriculum offered more than mere "professional training." Instead, it also aimed to instill in its students an appreciation for the "dignity of labor" and for the connection between the spirit and the soil that that labor was to help cultivate.[26]

For students like Nkrumah, who reflected relatively fondly on his time at Achimota, the new school's curriculum proved both challenging and rewarding. In his account, Nkrumah emphasized both the discipline and structure of Achimota life. As he recalled, house-masters tended to have wide-reaching powers in terms of disciplining their charges. Moreover, he insisted that his housemaster in Aggrey House was particularly harsh, specifically when it came to issues of attendance and timeliness for Sunday chapel. Students who failed to attend the service or missed the roll call would receive a set of vicious verbal assaults that, according to the future Ghanaian president, struck like "whiplashes" to one's ego and morale. Similar to Aggrey, Nkrumah also emphasized the importance of manual labor to Achimota life. However, in contrast to Aggrey, Nkrumah did not necessarily accent the supposed spiritual and character-building dimensions of the school's focus on labor. Instead, Nkrumah presented such work in part as a disciplinary tool, recounting how, after arriving late to chapel one Sunday, the Aggrey House headmaster punished him by providing him with "a large plot of ground to weed."[27]

Much like his previous account of his primary education in Half Assini, Nkrumah asserted that over the duration of his tenure at Achimota he ultimately came to appreciate the rigor and even discipline of the institution. Moreover, Nkrumah similarly reminisced on the religious and cultural dimensions of the curriculum. Both drumming and dancing featured prominently in Nkrumah's reflections on his and his peers' experiences at Achimota. Both arts served as extracurricular yet compulsory features of the school's curriculum.[28] In the case of Nkrumah, he noted how the school's focus on dancing in particular had provided him an opportunity to further connect with other Fante and Nzema students as they created a dance troupe of their own. Nkrumah also recalled his experiences acting at Achimota, playing, for instance, the title role in a production that emphasized key themes of education, science, rationality, and imperial connection and mobility through the character Nkrumah portrayed. At the heart of the play, Nkrumah recounted in his autobiography, were the lessons Nkrumah's character brought back to the Gold Coast after returning from abroad in England, as his character utilized "his scientific knowledge . . . [to] outwit superstition and witchcraft." Nkrumah would also partake in a number of sports during his time at Achimota, focusing on track and field (athletics) and the sprinting events specifically, as well as hone his future public-speaking skills through a student-organized speech-making club—the Aggrey Students' Society.[29]

In contrast to the school's cultural curriculum, however, Nkrumah struggled with his religious education at Achimota. Whereas in his childhood at Half Assini he had become an enthusiastic and active participant in the church, he suggested that his time at Achimota was one in which he increasingly began to question key aspects of organized religion and specifically the obligatory nature of religious education, chapel, and religious reflection demanded of Achimota's students. Nkrumah even claimed that he went so far as to regularly skip the school's mandatory church services and advocate to the church and school leaders for an end to the obligation of church attendance.[30] As Nkrumah grew older, his connection to organized religion would continue to wane, leading him in 1957 to declare himself "a nondenominational Christian and a Marxist socialist," while insisting that he had "not found any contradiction between the two."[31] Despite his religious struggles, however, Nkrumah noted that both his fellow students and instructors recognized his potential during his time at Achimota, choosing him as prefect during his final year at the institution.[32]

* * *

Kwame Nkrumah graduated from Achimota in 1930. In the years following his tenure at the school, the future Ghanaian president moved between a number of teaching positions in the western and central Gold Coast. In many ways, Nkrumah's experiences in the early twentieth-century Gold Coast were exceptional. His ability to attend primary school in Half Assini distinguished him from many of his peers, and his enrollment at Achimota was beyond fortuitous. Furthermore, his encounters with figures like J. E. K. Aggrey encouraged him to look to the United States as an opportunity to continue his education—a prospect that very few Gold Coasters in the 1920s and 1930s could even contemplate.[33]

However, the generalities of Nkrumah's experiences during his youth and young adulthood were shared by many others of his generation, as an increasing number of Gold Coast youth and their families negotiated the rapidly changing world around them in the late nineteenth and early twentieth centuries. This was a period of intense and unpredictable transition culminating in the creation of the Gold Coast colonial state in the latter decades of the nineteenth century. Not only was this colonial incursion disruptive to the region's many different traditional states, but, combined with the rise of new export-oriented cash-crop industries, it helped transform Gold Coast social and cultural life. By the time of Nkrumah's birth, Gold Coasters faced an increasingly professionalized and consolidated colonial state that forced them into new forms of negotiation and experimentation. For many families like Nkrumah's, schooling thus quickly emerged as the social and cultural scaffolding of this transition as it acculturated Gold Coast young people in many of the values of the colonial regime, while simultaneously opening for some new networks of opportunity, engagement, and experimentation—political, intellectual, and professional—that at various times worked within and beyond the Gold Coast educational system's colonial and imperial roots.

3

Diasporic Connections and Anticolonial Experimentation

To read Kwame Nkrumah's autobiography, the years following his time at Achimota were ones of self-exploration and personal growth. As a teacher, Nkrumah worked in several different institutions during the early 1930s, beginning his career in the now Central Region town of Elmina. As the site of the Portuguese arrival in the Gold Coast in the late fifteenth century and, later, the capital of the Dutch presence in the region, Elmina had long represented a cosmopolitan hub within the Gold Coast. In Elmina, Nkrumah taught in the town's Roman Catholic Junior School, largely focusing his attention on the school's youngest children. After a year in Elmina, Nkrumah was offered the position of "head teacher" further west in Axim's Roman Catholic Junior School before eventual transfer to Amissano. Like Elmina, Axim had been a prominent trading center during the precolonial era, focused first on trade with the Portuguese and subsequently the Dutch. Also like Elmina, the slave trade eventually became a key component of Axim's economy. For Nkrumah in the early 1930s, part of the allure of the position in Axim, however, was almost certainly its proximity to his birthplace, being approximately twenty-five kilometers east of Nkroful and less than a hundred from where he grew up in Half Assini. During his time in Axim, Nkrumah was also quite active beyond his teaching responsibilities as he formed the Nzima Literature Association and began preparations to take the London Matriculation, a school-leaving exam required for admittance to British university-level education. Nkrumah noted in his autobiography that when he took the matriculation, however, he would ultimately fail the Latin and mathematics exams.[1]

As Nkrumah additionally recounted in his autobiography, his time in Axim also represented his first serious introduction into Gold Coast politics. Active in Axim's social and cultural scene upon coming to the now Western Region town in 1932, it was not long after arriving in Axim that Nkrumah came into contact with S. R. Wood, the secretary of the National Congress of British West Africa (NCBWA). According to Nkrumah, he and Wood would spend many hours discussing the Gold Coast past together, with Wood educating the young Nkrumah on the history of the colony's political activism. As secretary of the NCBWA, Wood, for his part, was himself a key figure in this history. Formed in 1920 by a group of Anglophone West Africans from the Gold Coast, Nigeria, Sierra Leone, and the Gambia with the prominent Gold Coast nationalist J. E. Casely Hayford as its president, the NCBWA not only sought to advocate for the rights of African subjects under British colonial rule, but, in doing so, simultaneously began cultivating a broader idea of a shared pan–West African political identity in the British colonial sphere. Writing in the Nigerian newspaper, *West African Nationhood,* for instance, J. C. Zizer—a key figure in the Nigerian National Democratic Party—argued that the goal of the NCBWA should not be understood in the context of "the narrow limits of Party Politics." Instead, he presented the objectives of the organization as ultimately aligned to "the greater and more envious pretention of [West African] Nationhood [*sic*]."[2]

It is difficult to ascertain what exactly Nkrumah took away from his conversations with Wood. Moreover, by the early 1930s, much of the momentum behind the NCBWA had begun to wane, catalyzed in part by Casely Hayford's 1930 death. However, throughout the early 1930s the Gold Coast remained a site of intense and expanding political activity. Harkening back to the Gold Coast's long tradition of print activism, new newspapers rapidly emerged on the colony's political scene during the period, challenging the colonial state and its policies in new ways. In doing so, they created spaces for a new generation of Gold Coast activists to find a voice on the colony's political stage. In 1931, for instance, Nkrumah's future rival and a key individual involved in encouraging him to return to the Gold Coast in 1947, J. B.

Danquah, would found the *West African Times* (later, the *Times of West Africa*) in Accra. Versatile, the *Times of West Africa* combined regular critiques of the colonial government with engaging human-interest stories, including future Nkrumah-ally Mabel Dove's widely popular, pseudonymously authored "Women's/Ladies' Corner," to draw a wider and more diverse audience to the colony's press. Similarly, in 1934, Nnamdi Azikiwe, the Nigerian nationalist and Lincoln University alum who Nkrumah would first meet shortly thereafter, took over the editorship of the Accra-based *African Morning Post*.[3] For the next three years, under Azikiwe's leadership, the *African Morning Post* conducted an unceasing assault on the colonial government in its pages, inviting the ire of the government and ultimately leading to its attempted prosecution of Azikiwe under the colony's sedition law and his eventual return to Nigeria.

Listening to Wood's account of the Gold Coast's political history, Nkrumah surely would have connected his elder's tales with the growing activism he witnessed developing in the Gold Coast around him. Moreover, Nkrumah credited Wood with helping him make his way to the United States to continue his education. With no university-level institutions in the Gold Coast at the time, Gold Coasters seeking such a degree had little choice but to go abroad for higher-level study. However, for a subject of the British Empire like Nkrumah, the decision to consider the United States for such study was not an obvious one. In the imperial context of the Gold Coast as well as elsewhere in British West Africa, most viewed an American education as significantly less prestigious than one pursued in the metropole itself. Moreover, the logistics of admission to an American university and even getting to the United States for a colonial subject were far from straightforward. Cost, though, would prove Nkrumah's most immediate obstacle to his education, requiring him to approach relatives and others in his community for help in securing the necessary funds for his travel. Nevertheless, Nkrumah set off for the United States in October 1935, traveling via Great Britain. In the United States, the future Ghanaian president was to attend Lincoln University, a small historically Black institution in rural Pennsylvania.[4] Nkrumah would ultimately spend more than a decade abroad, both in the United States and Great Britain. It was during this time that much of the future president's political and social thought began to take shape and mature. As a result, Nkrumah's political and intellectual growth would in turn be fundamentally cultivated through the changing diasporic and global contexts—the Depression-era and wartime United States, American Black radical politics, and the anticolonial and pan-African networks of the postwar United Kingdom—that marked his time in the diaspora.

* * *

In one of the more memorable, possibly dramatized, episodes of Nkrumah's 1957 autobiography, Nkrumah described his emotions walking down the streets of London in October 1935 and reading from the newspaper headlines that Italy had attacked Ethiopia, the only precolonial African state to have survived the nineteenth-century Scramble for Africa without being colonized. Nkrumah had recently arrived in London in the midst of the attack to wait for a visa for his travel to the United States. As a British subject without access to an American consulate in West Africa, such an interlude was unavoidable. It was an interlude that, according to him, fundamentally reshaped his understanding of colonialism. As he writes in the autobiography, all he saw was the newspapers' banners, yet he quickly became overwhelmed by emotion. "That was all I needed," he steadfastly recalled. "At that moment it was almost as if the whole of London had suddenly declared war on me personally." Continuing, he explained that "for the next few minutes, I could do nothing but glare at each impassive face wondering if those people could possibly realize the wickedness of colonialism, and praying that the day might come when I could play my part in bringing about the downfall of such a system." As a result, Nkrumah, in that moment, declared to himself that he "was ready and willing to go through hell itself . . . in order to achieve my object."[5]

Nkrumah was not alone in detailing the political and cultural significance of the Italian invasion of Ethiopia for peoples of African descent living inside and outside the continent. In the United States, for instance, the invasion galvanized groups of African American communists fighting in the Spanish Civil War to turn their fight against Spanish fascism into a proxy war against Italian fascism.[6] Likewise, the Trinidadian pan-African Marxist C. L. R. James emphasized the role of the invasion in unsettling colonial governments in the British West Indies as it accentuated racial tensions within the islands during the mid-1930s.[7] Furthermore, committees and activist organizations in cities ranging from New York to Paris to Accra to Lagos held meetings, collected money and other resources, demonstrated, and organized locally and internationally in support for the Ethiopian cause.[8] Meanwhile, C. L. R. James and Amy Ashwood Garvey would form the International African Friends of Ethiopia (IAFE) in 1935. George Padmore, a prominent Trinidadian Marxist journalist who would later become one of Nkrumah's most important mentors, joined the organization shortly after as the IAFE sought to protest and organize against the Italian invasion.[9] Similarly, in the Gold Coast, the *Gold Coast Spectator* insisted that each Gold Coaster, "down to the schoolboy, knows he has everything in common with the Ethiopians."[10]

For Nkrumah, the invasion set the tone for his arrival in the diaspora. Arriving on the Lincoln University campus in late 1935, Nkrumah found an institution with a long history of educating and training African students. Founded in 1854 as the United States' first institution of higher education devoted to the education of Black students, many of the school's first students became American-born emigrants to the newly independent, African American–founded republic of Liberia. By as early as 1872, the school had extended its reach into Liberia beyond the republic's prominent and politically influential Americo-Liberian community. This included, among others, the admission of ten students from the country's indigenous population. In 1896, two students from South Africa would join the school. By 1923, an additional twenty-one South Africans would graduate from Lincoln.[11] In 1929, Nnamdi Azikiwe would arrive at Lincoln, coming from a previous stint at Howard University in Washington, DC. At Lincoln, Azikiwe participated in a variety of school clubs and activities while also honing his journalistic voice writing for two prominent African American newspapers, the *Baltimore Afro-American* and the *Philadelphia Tribune.* As Lincoln's first Black president, Horace Mann Bond, reflected in 1976, Lincoln had a profound influence on the future Nigerian agitator and eventual president as it provided him the space to learn that "a black man could talk back to a white man."[12]

The lessons Azikiwe learned at Lincoln drove his activism once he returned to West Africa and particularly in his journalistic endeavors in the Gold Coast. When Nkrumah first encountered Azikiwe in the mid-1930s, Azikiwe encouraged the young Gold Coast teacher to look toward Lincoln as he prepared to study abroad. Azikiwe would eventually offer to write a letter of recommendation for Nkrumah in 1935 to help secure his admittance to the school.[13]

At Lincoln, Nkrumah—like Azikiwe before him—embedded himself in the social life of the campus, taking part in speech-making contests and earning money by working in the dining hall and as a library assistant. He also wrote in his autobiography of how he would earn additional pocket money by writing reports for fellow students who "grudged having to spend their spare time writing them up." According to him, he would earn a dollar per report, thus allowing him to raise "quite a few dollars towards my out-of-pocket expenses."[14] During his time at Lincoln, Nkrumah also pledged the prominent African American fraternity Phi Beta Sigma. In joining Phi Beta Sigma, Nkrumah again followed in Azikiwe's footsteps, for Azikiwe had joined the fraternity's Howard University chapter prior to arriving at Lincoln.[15] In his autobiography, Nkrumah emphasized the process of his initiation into the fraternity, including having his "trousers . . . ripped off in front of everyone," being chased by hounds, and beatings. Yet fraternity life surely offered him more than the indignity of hazing. Rather, it bound him to a community of brothers that he would carry throughout his time at Lincoln, providing perspectives on and connections to African American life and culture to which few Gold Coasters of the era had access.[16]

Beyond campus life, Lincoln also provided Nkrumah with a base through which to explore the social, cultural, and political diversity of the Depression-era and wartime United States. For Nkrumah, the scarcity caused by both the global depression and the Second World War indelibly marked his time in the United States. In the Gold Coast, the depression had led to the plummeting of the colony's various export commodities, including most importantly cocoa. Between the 1929–30 and 1930–31 fiscal years, for instance, the price per ton of cocoa paid to farmers more than halved, bottoming out two years later at £11 per ton.[17] Gold Coast farmers responded to the cocoa market's collapse by seeking to withhold their cocoa from the market, unleashing a series of hold-ups that would emerge as a defining feature of depression-era Gold Coast popular politics. Over the course of the 1930s, the cocoa hold-ups would receive regular attention from the colony's various African-run newspapers, including Azikiwe's *African Morning Post*. At the heart of the farmers' and African-run newspapers' protests was what they presented as the inherent unfairness of a global cocoa market in which pricing was set exclusively at the point of consumption for African-produced goods and at the point of production for the sale of goods imported into Africa. "If the African consumer must be prepared to purchase foreign goods at the price asked for by the foreign producer," the *African Morning Post* asked in October 1937, "is there any reason why the foreign consumer should not be made to purchase African goods at the price demanded by the African producer?"[18]

To Nkrumah in the early 1930s, just out of Achimota at the time, the complex linkages between the economic collapse in the United States, followed by Europe, to the political economy of the Gold Coast may not have been entirely visible to him. Even the realities of the hardships faced by the colony's cocoa producers during the period may have only existed in the abstract for the young teacher as he began his career in Elmina—a site far from the colony's most vibrant cocoa-producing regions to the north and east of the coastal town. Instead, Nkrumah likely followed the changes in the Gold Coast cocoa market via newspapers like the *African Morning Post*. For the colony's farmers, though, the collapse of the international and, by extension, local markets led to a state of increasing indebtedness as they sought to cope with the effects of both the market's extremely low prices and their boycotts of those prices.[19] Additionally, for those who labored on the cocoa farms, the cocoa collapse of the 1930s also led to a possible revival in various forms of social dependency in the colony's prominent cocoa-growing regions, most notably in Asante.[20]

The scene in the United States for Nkrumah would have been much more visceral, especially when he traveled beyond the Lincoln campus. Although he does not comment on them directly in his autobiography, it is difficult to imagine that the breadlines and tent cities, which have become icons of the Depression-era United States, would have been unfamiliar to the young Gold Coaster, especially in his excursions to nearby Philadelphia and New York. As songwriter E. Y. Harburg explained in Stud Terkel's oral history of the Depression, while walking down the streets in New York "you'd see the bread lines. . . . Fellows with burlap on their shoes were lined up all around Columbus Circle, and went for blocks and blocks around the park, waiting."[21] Meanwhile, in certain working-class neighborhoods in Philadelphia, more than 25 percent of families had a head of household who was unemployed, with another 25 percent having one underemployed by as early as 1930. By 1934, approximately two years before a young Nkrumah would have begun familiarizing himself with the city, more than three hundred thousand of the city's residents had registered with the state of Pennsylvania as unemployed.[22] As a result, W. E. B. Du Bois would argue in 1939 that at the heart of the Depression was a fundamental shift in the American psyche, as the realities of the Depression sapped the nation of its optimism. Poverty, hunger, and insecurity had become the new normal for many American families. "In other words," Du Bois explained, "the nation has met Poverty the Stranger," and, as opposed to sending this stranger on his way, it had "begun to inquire about his ancestry and search his stature and lineaments so as never again to forget him or ignore him."[23]

Moreover, for the Black communities within New York and Philadelphia with which Nkrumah would have interacted most, the Depression affected them disproportionately. In Philadelphia, for instance, the city's Black population had skyrocketed in the decades preceding the 1930s Depression, with Du Bois—who in 1899 had undertaken one of the first sociological studies of the city's Black population—estimating it at nearly 40,000 people in 1890.[24] By 1916, the population had reached more than 130,000 and, by 1929, just under 220,000.[25] The contraction of the labor market with the Depression devastated the Black community. By 1931, the Black unemployment rate had grown to 35 percent. A year later, the Black labor market bottomed out, leaving 56 percent of the city's Black population without work.[26] In New York, Black workers faced similar circumstances. In Harlem specifically, Black unemployment was up to three times the rate of whites throughout the rest of the city during the 1930s. As a result, the neighborhood's residents faced regular evictions, the loss of their savings, and, for those who owned businesses, the loss of their businesses as Black wealth and ownership in the neighborhood collapsed over the decade. Furthermore, Black-owned or managed real estate dropped from 35 percent to 5 percent in the neighborhood between 1929 and 1935, while additional declines accompanied Black-owned retail spaces.[27] The result was a situation in both cities where the Depression left Black communities in a persistent state of precarity throughout the 1930s and into the 1940s.

Nkrumah himself was not immune to the effects of the Depression. Reflecting on the Depression for his Ghanaian audience in 1957, Nkrumah described the scenes he had seen on the American streets. "Life was so hard on some people," he wrote in his autobiography, "that sometimes I would see men and women picking scraps of food from out of the dustbins." He then added, "In fact, had it not been for the generosity of my landlady, I should have been doing the same thing."[28] As a student, summer vacations proved particularly difficult for him as he sought to stay afloat financially while Lincoln closed. As he recounted in his autobiography, he spent part of his first summer vacation in Harlem working as a fishmonger. Buying fish each morning, Nkrumah and a Sierra Leonean friend would occupy the rest of the day trying to sell off their wares. Not only did Nkrumah quickly find this business unprofitable, but, he reported, it also severely affected his health as he broke out in rashes due to an apparent allergy to the fish. Nkrumah next turned to employment in a soap factory. Describing what he presented as the worst job he would ever have, Nkrumah told of how trucks would dump "rotting entrails and lumps of fat of animals" outside the factory, making it his job to transport the animal parts to the processing plant via wheelbarrow. As with the fish, Nkrumah quickly encountered health problems while working in the soap factory, forcing him to abandon the position for a job waiting tables on a ship traveling between New York and Veracruz, Mexico.[29]

As Nkrumah negotiated the social and economic realities of the Depression during his first years in the United States, he also sought to take part in the changing politics of the American Black community of the interwar years. In both Philadelphia and New York,

Black politics had radicalized over the course of the first decades of the twentieth century. In the 1920s, Harlem, where Nkrumah would live and work a decade later, had famously emerged as the epicenter for Black culture and politics in the United States, drawing artists, musicians, intellectuals, and activists to the northern Manhattan neighborhood. In addition, the rise in the neighborhood of the Universal Negro Improvement Association (UNIA)—originally founded in Kingston, Jamaica, in 1914—in the late teens and early 1920s further centered Harlem within the broader political imagination. Headed by the Jamaican activist Marcus Garvey, the UNIA's Harlem branch, like most branches throughout the UNIA's global network, established an array of social services including funeral insurance, medical clinics, and employment opportunities as well as hosting social events like dances and concerts, all designed to promote Black self-reliance.[30] It was also from Harlem that Garvey established the UNIA's shipping line, the Black Star Line, which would inspire Nkrumah's own vision for a Ghanaian shipping company following Ghana's independence. Meanwhile, in Philadelphia, UNIA meetings would draw crowds of up to six thousand people and bring in many of the city's most prominent clergy members in UNIA leadership roles.[31] As one former Philadelphia-based UNIA leader would explain in a 1940 interview, the ethos underlying the UNIA and drawing people to the organization was one of patient self-reliance as Black communities waited for the ideal moment to strike out on their own. To this end, he declared that "if we can solve our economic problem, then to hell with the white man."[32]

By the onset of the Depression in 1929, the formal apparatus of the Garveyist movement would endure considerable stress. In the UNIA specifically, Garvey's 1923 arrest and 1927 deportation from the United States severely weakened the organization. Further tempering the movement was the economic strain placed upon the UNIA due to the extravagance of its many projects, including the Black Star Line. However, in spite of Garvey's personal and the UNIA's institutional troubles in the mid- to late 1920s, Garveyism's spread throughout the United States, the Caribbean, and into Africa drew the attention of some of the Gold Coast's most prominent intellectuals of the period. Writing in 1925, for instance, Kobina Sekyi—a lawyer, writer, and key figure in both of the Gold Coast's most prominent early twentieth-century nationalist organizations (the Aborigines' Rights Protection Society and the NCBWA)—struggled with the meaning of Garveyism for Africa in an unpublished manuscript. At one level, Sekyi rejected Garvey's proposal to repatriate diasporic Africans back to the continent as at best naïve, arguing instead that "the salvation of the Africans in the world cannot but be most materially assisted by the Africans in America but must be controlled and directed from African Africa and by thoroughly African Africans." What Garveyism did offer, however, Sekyi argued, was a way of marrying what he presented as the materialism of Booker T. Washington with the idealism of W. E. B. Du Bois in African American politics.[33]

The specter of Garveyism proved foundational to Nkrumah's political and intellectual development. As he outlines in his autobiography, Nkrumah's initial introduction to Garveyism came through Garvey's own writings, most notably his *The Philosophy and Opinions of Marcus Garvey*. Published a little more than a decade prior to Nkrumah's arrival in the United States, *The Philosophy and Opinions* offered a collection of speeches and writings by the UNIA leader compiled, as Garvey biographer Colin Grant describes, to create a relatively "unthreatening apologia [of Garvey's thought] to white America." As Grant explains, the Garvey of *The Philosophy and Opinions* was thus a highly tempered Garvey.[34] Despite such a softening of the Jamaican's message, Nkrumah still saw in Garvey's work a message of self-sufficiency and self-determination that would serve as a cornerstone of his political and social thought throughout his lifetime. Moreover, as Nkrumah read widely during his time in the United States, he worked to weave his understanding of Garvey's message into his similar readings of a range of other major political and intellectual thinkers from the nineteenth and early twentieth centuries, including Georg Hegel, Karl Marx, Friedrich Engels, Vladimir Lenin, and Giuseppe Mazzini.[35] As with many of his contemporaries studying the political and social context of the early twentieth century, Marx,

Engels, and Lenin in particular joined Garvey in providing Nkrumah with a model through which to embark upon a formal critique of the colonial system in Africa and beyond—and, more fundamentally, save Garvey, the capitalist system that underpinned it. Lenin's 1917 *Imperialism: The Highest Stage of Capitalism* specifically would serve as the inspiration for two of Nkrumah's major works, *Towards Colonial Freedom* (1947) and *Neo-colonialism: The Last Stage of Imperialism* (1965).[36] Meanwhile, Mazzini's writings offered Nkrumah a language in which to reflect on questions of "nation" and "nationalism" in a comparative sense and thus begin the political and intellectual process of adapting them to an African colonial setting.

For Nkrumah, his time in the United States was thus a period of political and intellectual exploration. In 1939, Nkrumah completed his degree at Lincoln University, graduating with degrees in economics and sociology. Following his time as an undergraduate student at Lincoln, Nkrumah accepted a post teaching philosophy at the school before entering Lincoln's seminary and then a master's program at the University of Pennsylvania in Philadelphia. Before and after the United States' entry into the Second World War in December 1941, Nkrumah would continue to seek out opportunities to integrate himself deeper into key sites of Black culture and politics in the country, including Black churches, Paul Robeson's Council on African Affairs, and the National Association for the Advancement of Colored

People, among others.[37] In doing so, Nkrumah not only sought to build relationships and reflect on this unique and eclectic collection of political and social networks, but also, by taking and adapting what he witnessed in the United States, to begin to the lay the political and intellectual groundwork for his future activism in Great Britain and the Gold Coast.

* * *

Kwame Nkrumah left the United States for Great Britain approximately a decade after he arrived. Reaching London in the early summer months of 1945, Nkrumah found a city devastated by the war. He also found a city with a continuous and vibrant Black political culture that in various incarnations dates back to at least the sixteenth century.[38] Prior to the end of the nineteenth century, much of London's Black community's political attention centered on the politics of antislavery. By the early twentieth century, as the city's Black community had begun to grow with the increasing arrival of West African and Caribbean students and workers, the politics of the community also began to diversify to include broader critiques of the British imperial government.[39]

By Nkrumah's 1945 arrival in the city, a substantial infrastructure had emerged to support African newcomers. Organizations like the West African Student Union (WASU), founded in the mid-1920s, combined a clear pan-African mission tied to the promotion of African history and culture with a hostel system designed to provide the city's newest West African arrivals with a community and a safe and secure place to stay upon arriving in the imperial capital. WASU was also a place where Gold Coasters in particular had made their mark on the city's Black culture, with J. B. Danquah serving as the organization's first president. By the 1940s, numerous individuals who would become key figures on the Gold Coast/Ghanaian political stage of the 1950s and 1960s would make their way through the organization. Describing WASU in his 1990 autobiography, Joe Appiah presented the organization as at once a community of West Africans intently interested in debating the future of colonialism in Africa and a quasi–social club committed to helping its members navigate the social and economic realities of life in Britain.[40] Appiah himself would serve as WASU's president for five years, during which time he would befriend Nkrumah—a friendship that would last into the mid-1950s when Appiah broke from Nkrumah's Convention People's Party to join the newly formed opposition party, the National Liberation Movement. Nkrumah would eventually imprison Appiah.

For Nkrumah in 1945, however, his arrival in the United Kingdom was one foremost marked by excitement. Upon Nkrumah's arrival in London, the prominent pan-Africanist George Padmore met him at the train station and immediately transported him to the WASU hostel, where Nkrumah based himself as he sought more permanent housing.[41] The relationship between Padmore and Nkrumah would be a lasting one, surviving until Padmore's abrupt death in September 1959. In the early 1950s, Padmore would visit Nkrumah in Accra and advise the then Gold Coast prime minister as he and his government planned the colony's path toward self-government. Following independence, Nkrumah would name Padmore his advisor on African affairs, with Padmore taking a lead role in organizing two of the Nkrumah era's highest-profile pan-African events: the April 1958 Conference of Independent African States and the December 1958 All-African Peoples' Conference (see chapter 4). Furthermore, Padmore would help transform Ghana into a center for anticolonial activism in the months leading up to his death as he recruited African students in the United Kingdom to come to Ghana and continue their education.[42]

For politically active Africans like Nkrumah during the interwar and early postwar years, Padmore, through his writings, would have been a very familiar figure. In the 1920s, Padmore was active in the Black internationalist scene of New York, recruiting for the American Communist Party and writing for the *Negro Champion*. In 1930, he left the United States for Moscow. Inspired by the anticolonial turn of the Comintern in the late 1920s, Padmore would spend three years going between Moscow and Hamburg and editing the Soviet-sponsored *Negro Worker,* before his arrest by the new Nazi government in Germany and eventual break with the Soviet

Union and the Comintern in 1933. In the following years, Padmore would reestablish himself in the United Kingdom while regularly writing for a number of prominent West African newspapers, including Nnamdi Azikiwe's *African Morning Post* and his Lagos-based *West African Pilot* as well as, in the Gold Coast, the Kumasi-based *Ashanti Pioneer*. In the United States, Nkrumah would have likely gained familiarity with Padmore via his additional writings in many of the country's most important Black newspapers, such as the *New York Amsterdam News,* the *Baltimore Afro-American,* the *Pittsburgh Courier,* and the *Chicago Defender.*[43]

By the time of Nkrumah's arrival in London in mid-1945, Padmore and others had begun to turn their attention to the question of what the postwar world would look like. As Nkrumah would allude to in his autobiography by noting how Britain's wartime paper rations had famished the country's newspapers, the scars of the war were ubiquitous in Londoners' daily lives. Even in these last days of the war, rationing, the memories of the German bombing campaigns, and the instability the war had instilled in the British political system were fundamental parts of life within the city.[44] Padmore, for his part, adopted the uncertainty of the moment as an opportunity to challenge and reimagine the world system. Writing in October 1945 in the *West African Pilot,* Padmore documented the diplomatic attempts taking place in Europe and the United States to ensure sustained northern control over the European powers'

African colonies. In doing so, the Trinidadian characterized these efforts as a new Berlin Conference, referencing the 1884–85 conference at which Europe's major powers divided Africa among themselves for colonization.[45] Two years later, in the *Ashanti Pioneer*, Padmore would return to this theme as he called out a collection of leftists within the British Labour Party for advocating what he presented as a policy of "united European exploitation of Africa." Viewing the Middle East colonies as a lost cause, this group within the Labour Party, who Padmore snidely mentioned understood themselves as socialists, presented Africa as the site to which Europe's colonial powers should turn their attention for "the next twenty more years"—a prospect Padmore considered absurd as "everywhere . . . [people] are demanding, and in many cases fighting with arms in hand, for their long over due [*sic*] freedom."[46]

As early as February 1945, Padmore had begun to make formal arrangements for a possible pan-African conference in order to address Africa's and the Caribbean's place in the anticipated postwar world. Following his midyear arrival in London, Nkrumah dove into Padmore's planning, taking a prominent role in the organization of what would become the Fifth Pan-African Congress, held in Manchester in October 1945. In contrast to the previous Pan-African Congresses largely organized by W. E. B. Du Bois in the decade following the First World War, the Manchester Congress explicitly centered its debates on pathways to colonial self-determination. Much like during the First World War a generation earlier, the question of self-determination dominated the Second World War. As viewed by the Allied powers during the early stages of the war, the Axis powers' foremost political crime was their disrespect for the sovereignty and political wishes of the territories they invaded. Accentuating this belief in their August 1941 Atlantic Charter, the American president Franklin Roosevelt and the British prime minister Winston Churchill—in many ways echoing their predecessors two decades earlier—declared the universality of a people's right "to choose the form of government under which they will live."[47] However, shortly after the declaration, Churchill again followed his predecessors' lead as he quickly sought to affirm that the principles outlined in the charter did not apply to Britain's colonies.

Almost immediately, however, West African news-papers, activists, and others had begun to push back against British attempts to read colonial peoples out of the charter. For them, not only did these efforts lift the veil off the colonial project in Africa and else-where, but, in doing so, further spotlighted the impe-rial doublespeak of Churchill and others who sought to de-universalize the expressed universal ideals of demo-cratic self-determination they accorded to those living in Europe.[48] In 1949, for instance, Nnamdi Azikiwe, whose *West African Pilot* had been at the forefront of the anticolonial critiques of the British reading of the charter, summed up the arguments against the British interpretation of the document. In doing so, he argued that such a rendering of the charter fundamentally represented an imperial doubling down on "a political theory, which seems to be an exclusive property of the good peoples of Europe and America, whose rulers appear to find war a profitable mission and enterprise."[49]

When the Pan-African Congress met in Manchester in October 1945, organizers and attendees did not view their debates over self-determination in isolation. Rather, they interrogated the ways in which the narrower question of self-determination illuminated the broader issue of colonialism writ large, for the failures of the colonial powers to take seriously—or even consider—colonized Africans' and others' claims to the right of self-determination had made clear the bankruptcy of the colonial project itself. As a result, the congress's delegates, including Nkrumah, demanded an immediate end to colonial rule within Africa and beyond. To this end, the delegates specifically emphasized "the right of all peoples to govern themselves" in their "Declaration to the Colonial Workers, Farmers, and Intellectuals," while also stressing that this right included the "right of all Colonial peoples to control their own destiny." Colonialism in all its forms was at its heart an exploitative project, they argued, and any extension of the rights of self-determination or self-governance to colonized peoples necessarily undermined the colonial project as a whole. For this reason, the delegates called upon all colonized peoples to organize themselves against the colonial system and be willing to "fight for these ends by all the means at their disposal," including the use of strikes and boycotts against the colonial administration.[50]

In a declaration addressed to the colonial powers specifically, the congress's delegates again outlined their desire to see an end to colonial rule on the continent. "We," they asserted, "are determined to be free." Moreover, as they continued, they alluded to the many ways in which the colonial powers had long betrayed the promises of colonial rule over the previous decades. Ostensibly predicated on liberal promises of education, modern healthcare, the extension of democratic values, and free trade, colonialism as advertised had been presented as a project of social and cultural uplift in both Europe and Africa. On the ground, however, more than a generation of activists and others had pointed to not only the colonial powers' failures to live up to these pledges, but also the ways in which those administering the colonial system itself had actively sought to stifle political, social, and cultural expression within Europe's African colonies and thwart African attempts to secure a better life for themselves. Furthermore, at the root of the colonial problem, the declaration continued, was the broader global economic system colonialism supported: monopoly capitalism. It was monopoly capital's necessarily accumulative nature that buttressed and stimulated the colonial government's exploitation of colonized peoples.

As a result, as part of their demand for an end to colonial rule in Africa and beyond, the Manchester delegates also called for a complete reorganization of the global economic system as they presented "economic democracy as the only real democracy."[51]

Nkrumah himself took credit for drafting the congress's "Declaration to the Colonial Workers, Farmers, and Intellectuals," while attributing the "Declaration to the Colonial Powers" to Du Bois.[52] In his own address to the congress, Nkrumah would develop many of the ideas articulated in the declarations even further as he undertook an economic analysis of the necessarily exploitative nature of the colonial system in the global economy. Furthermore, he would insist that such a system was at the root of each of the two world wars in the first half of the twentieth century.[53]

Nkrumah would return to the ideas articulated at the Manchester Congress with the publication in 1947 of his first book, *Towards Colonial Freedom*. Published as a relatively short pamphlet, *Towards Colonial Freedom* stands out not for its originality, but for the ways in which it builds upon longstanding critiques of the colonial system coming from both within and outside of Africa. This Leninist-inspired text undertakes a systematic dissection of the role of capitalist extraction in its analysis of the rapacious nature of the European colonial system within Africa. Much as Lenin had argued nearly three decades earlier, Nkrumah opened his book by insisting that "the basis of colonial territorial dependence is economic." As outlined by Nkrumah, Europe's colonies fundamentally served as safety nets for the European economy itself. Not only did they provide the raw materials necessary for European industry to function, but they also served as new markets (in which Europeans sold goods manufactured out of Africa's raw materials) and as sites for European capital investment. To Nkrumah, echoing the declarations articulated in Manchester two years earlier, any attempt to disrupt this exploitation would necessarily require political action and independence.[54]

* * *

In the years following the Manchester Congress, Nkrumah maintained an active role in the British anticolonial scene. Coming out of the Manchester Congress itself, George Padmore, along with the Guyanese pan-Africanist T. Ras Makonnen, aimed to build upon the congress's momentum by using the Padmore-founded Pan-African Federation (PAF) to publicize the congress's declaration and resolutions. Like Padmore, Makonnen would later join Nkrumah's government following Ghana's 1957 independence. As Makonnen would explain in his autobiography, the PAF had been key in organizing the Manchester Congress and, in the years following the congress, building relationships and connections with political organizations and parties sympathetic to the African cause.[55] Meanwhile, Nkrumah joined many of the congress's West African delegates in establishing the West African National Secretariat (WANS), of which he would serve as the organization's general secretary. At the heart of the WANS was a reframing of the anti-colonial vision articulated by figures like Nkrumah at the Manchester Congress to the goal of West African independence and unification. Moreover, the WANS articulated its vision for West Africa in expressly socialist terms, with founding member Bankole Awooner-Renner advocating for a "West African Soviet Union."[56]

However, in late 1947 Nkrumah's work with the WANS was abruptly cut short when he was invited by the newly formed United Gold Coast Convention, spearheaded by the longtime Gold Coast nationalist and agitator J. B. Danquah, to return to the Gold Coast and become its first general secretary. After much debate, consultation, and apprehension, Nkrumah left the WANS and returned to the Gold Coast, arriving in the restive colony in December 1947 after more than twelve years abroad.

4

Between Nation and Pan-Africanism

Part I

Kwame Nkrumah's return to the Gold Coast in late 1947 was never a foregone conclusion. Working in London with the West African National Secretariat (WANS) and as part of George Padmore's broader circle of pan-African anticolonial activists, Nkrumah had positioned himself at the center of a vibrant movement aimed at radically transforming Africa's place within the world. In his role as secretary for the WANS, for instance, Nkrumah set out to organize African students and workers, plan conferences, and hold public demonstrations designed to educate the public to the exploitative nature of colonial rule and demand its end on the African continent. Similarly, as Nkrumah describes in his autobiography, he also came to lead a "vanguard group" of activists known as "the Circle." Modeled as a quasi–secret society, members of the Circle were "to train themselves in order to be able to commence revolutionary work."[1]

In the ensuing years, the Circle—more in its claimed existence than its actual activities—would draw significant consternation from colonial officials who sought to peg it and Nkrumah as little more than communist agitators aimed at disrupting the peace within Britain's African colonies, especially the Gold Coast.[2]

For Nkrumah, compared to what he believed he was building in London, the invitation from the United Gold Coast Convention (UGCC) to return to the Gold Coast and serve as the new organization's general secretary appeared underwhelming. The initial invitation came from a fellow Lincoln University alum, Ako Adjei. A lawyer who himself had recently returned to the Gold Coast, Adjei, like Nkrumah, represented a new generation of educated, mobile, and energetic leaders that elders in the newly formed UGCC believed would help build the organization and advance its broader quest to democratize the Gold Coast political system. In the colony, like elsewhere in Africa, the Second World War had coincided with a number of political and constitutional reforms, including attempts to Africanize the colony's Legislative Council. However, for many in the Gold Coast, particularly those in the colony's professional classes, the reforms did not go far enough. Instead, they argued that the reforms tended to elevate not the voices of these educated and rather cosmopolitan individuals, but rather those of the colony's chiefly class.[3] In response, the UGCC aimed to represent the voice of the Gold Coast middle classes on the colony's political stage, pushing for both further reform of the colony's political system and a broader recognition of a Gold Coast national identity.

The government initially saw the UGCC as a potential threat to the colony's political stability. Just several years earlier, in an attempt to secure greater funding and recognition for the Gold Coast from London, then governor Alan Burns had described the Gold Coast as a "model colony," a designation that stuck in popular understandings of the colony even if Burns himself would come to question its accuracy.[4] However, the government argued that the UGCC raised a number of threats to what it viewed as an already fragile colonial equilibrium. As understood by the colonial administration, the organization included a number of younger supporters who officials believed were inspired by the "violent nationalism and racialism" advocated by Nnamdi Azikiwe's newspapers in Lagos and that of the "nationalist movements in India, Burma, Ceylon [Sri Lanka] and elsewhere."[5] Yet for Nkrumah, the UGCC had set its sights too low in its political ambitions, leading him to initially demur at Adjei's invitation. Even more troubling for Nkrumah, as he would write a decade later in his autobiography, the movement as he saw it was not one of the people, but one, in his words, "backed almost entirely by reactionaries, middle-class lawyers and merchants" to whom his self-proclaimed "revolutionary background and ideas" would be anathema.[6]

However, after a period of contemplation, Nkrumah ultimately accepted the UGCC's offer to become its first general secretary. Setting sail for the Gold Coast in November, he arrived in the colony in December, stopping in Freetown, Sierra Leone, and Monrovia, Liberia, en route. In Freetown, a city long known as one of the intellectual hubs of Anglophone West Africa, Nkrumah met with the colony's most famous anticolonial activist, I. T. A. Wallace-Johnson, who served as president of the WANS and who, more than decade earlier, had been charged with sedition in the Gold Coast for an article he pseudonymously wrote for Azikiwe's *African Morning Post.* In Monrovia, Nkrumah sought but failed to secure an audience with Liberia's president, William Tubman. Nkrumah continued on to the Gold Coast port city of Takoradi, approximately seventy-five kilometers east of his hometown of Nkroful. Nkrumah would spend two weeks in the western Gold Coast reconnecting with his mother before traveling further east to Saltpond, where he would begin his work with the UGCC. From this small coastal town, Nkrumah would begin a political career that would give rise to one of Africa's first mass political parties and, over the course of the next eighteen years, push the boundaries of conventional definitions of the nation and nation-state as he sought to position an emergent Ghana at the center of a broader, transnational project of African liberation and unification.

* * *

The Gold Coast Nkrumah returned to in 1947 was a hub of excitement and unrest.[7] Economically, the

Second World War had transformed the opportunities available to many Gold Coasters. In the colony's urban centers in particular, inflation ran rampant throughout the war years and in the war's immediate aftermath, with the costs of some imported goods rising to more than eight times their prewar levels. The result was a tangible decline in real income for most individuals and families.[8] Elsewhere in the colony, wartime shortages of needed industrial commodities opened new opportunities and challenges for the colony's peoples. For instance, as historian Keri Lambert has shown, in the western Gold Coast, not far from where Nkrumah came of age, colonial officials sought to revive the region's previously abandoned rubber trade. For the British, the resurrection of the Gold Coast's rubber industry—with roots in the first decades of British colonial rule—promised the imperial government a new supply chain for this essential wartime commodity as it sought to replace the rubber supplies it had lost to the Japanese invasion of Southeast Asia during the war. For Gold Coasters living in the region, the abrupt restoration of its rubber trade created new opportunities for employment. However, as Lambert has detailed, much of this wartime employment took place under severe production pressures and in an environment of sustained efforts to depress worker payouts. By the end of the war, the Gold Coast rubber market would quickly collapse, leaving many of those involved in the trade bankrupt.[9]

The end of the Second World War also ushered in the demobilization of approximately seventy thousand Gold Coasters who had been recruited into the Gold Coast Regiment (GCR) of the Royal West African Frontier Force. Stationed in places ranging from the Gambia to North and East Africa to Southeast Asia, members of the GCR served the Allied forces by building roads, working as engineers, managing supply lines throughout the war, and engaging in combat.[10] Upon their return, the former soldiers sought work in an increasingly saturated labor market, leading to widespread unemployment and discontent throughout much of the colony. Further exacerbating the unrest within the ex-servicemen community were the inflationary pressures afflicting the colony, as its former soldiers watched their wartime savings plummet. Governmental attempts to alleviate some of the pressures on the colony's ex-servicemen through a range of social welfare initiatives and commemorative monuments failed to fully quell the discontent. In response, in 1946 a number of ex-servicemen would form the Gold Coast Ex-servicemen's Union, which over the ensuing years would advocate for a range of ex-servicemen's rights, including a greater governmental commitment to helping them find work and increases to their pensions.[11]

By the time of Nkrumah's arrival in December 1947, tensions in the colony had begun to boil over. In January 1948, a local Accra chief, Nii Kwabena Bonne III, sought to refocus the popular ire of the colony's peoples at the

Gold Coast's economic situation, targeting the colony's European and Levantine businesses with a boycott that would last through February. As businesses, African sellers, and consumers endured the effects of the boycott, the government agreed to a set of pricing concessions, which were to begin on February 28, allowing Nii Bonne to claim victory. Additionally, in February 1948, the Gold Coast Ex-servicemen's Union announced a march on the seat of the colonial government in Accra—Christiansborg (Osu) Castle, a seventeenth-century fort built for, among other things, the slave trade—to protest the ex-servicemen's treatment in the aftermath of the war. Scheduled for February 28, the day the boycott's pricing concessions were set to go into effect, approximately two thousand people—veterans and nonveterans alike—arrived to take part in the march on Christiansborg Castle. As the crowd deviated from the previously approved protest route, officers in the Gold Coast police force sought to draw the marchers back on course before opening fire on the unarmed crowd, killing two. Residents in Accra responded to the police shootings by taking to the streets and attacking foreign-owned businesses. Furthermore, as news of the events in Accra made its way to the Gold Coast's other major urban centers, riots broke out in many of these locales, including Koforidua and Kumasi, leaving several dead and many more injured.[12]

For Nkrumah, the political turmoil afflicting the Gold Coast in early 1948 appeared to offer a moment of opportunity in terms of how he read his role in the UGCC. As an organization, the UGCC's general leadership sought to take a cautious approach to the growing conflict in the colony. At the heart of the UGCC's broader political message was a desire to ensure an orderly and gradual extension of the right to self-determination and self-rule for the colony's peoples. Speaking at the UGCC's August 1947 founding, Danquah—the then doyen of Gold Coast nationalism—explained the new organization's mission as he described the Gold Coast's political position as one riven by insecurity and uncertainty. With the founding of the UGCC, Danquah asserted, "We have come to Saltpond to ponder and to deliberate upon the ways and means to bring an end to this insecurity and this frustration. British freedom," he continued, "is a precious thing. But British freedom is not Gold Coast freedom. British liberty is grand to have, but you cannot have and possess British liberty in a Gold Coast atmosphere. We must have, here and now, if we are to be well governed, a new kind of freedom, a Gold Coast freedom, a Gold Coast liberty."[13] To this end, the UGCC's general leadership envisioned its role as one of pressuring the colonial government into a set of constitutional reforms that would ensure an eventual path to Gold Coast self-determination under the leadership of the colony's educated elite, a class of Gold Coasters with a long history of nationalist political activity in the colony and one largely sidelined by the constitutional reforms that went into effect following the Second World War.

Inside the UGCC, Nkrumah struggled with the organization's leadership over what he viewed as its conservative response to the February disturbances. More broadly, he also questioned what he saw as the UGCC leadership's overly cautious approach to the question of African self-determination. Reflecting back on the arguments he and his colleagues had made approximately two years earlier at the Manchester Pan-African Congress, Nkrumah took a much more hardline view on the Gold Coast political situation, not only by demanding an immediate end to colonial rule within the colony, but by also vowing to replace Gold Coast colonialism with a political system framed around the interests and organization of the Gold Coast masses. For Nkrumah, the events of late February represented a popular rebuke of the UGCC leaders' caution and a simultaneous yearning for his vision of mass mobilization. To this end, he responded to the events without equivocation. Seemingly splitting from the UGCC's official line on the events as outlined in an eight-thousand-word cable written and disseminated by Danquah, Nkrumah wrote his own response. Moreover, he also circulated his response to an array of outlets on both sides of the burgeoning Cold War divide. Nkrumah's actions ultimately landed him as well as the UGCC's five other major figures—including Danquah—in detention on accusations of possibly instigating the February disturbances.[14] From the perspective of the colonial administration, Nkrumah's embrace of the February riots only further confirmed its previous

Figure 4.1. Kwame Nkrumah, ca. 1947. Photo reproduced courtesy of the United Kingdom's National Archives image library.

fears that he was little more than an agitator with supposed ambitions of introducing communism into the colony.[15]

Following Nkrumah's and his colleagues' release later that year, Nkrumah accelerated his mobilizing efforts, establishing his own newspaper—the *Accra Evening News*—in September 1948. In its opening issue, the *Evening News* sought to define itself firmly as the voice of African anticolonial agitation and mobilization in the Gold Coast. "Agitation is a common word now used by Crown Colony officials to brand those in the colonies who stem the spirit of colonial nationalism," the newspaper explained on September 3. "All leaders of West African political thought and action are stigmatized as agitators." However, "the true African nationalist . . . is not daunted by the term. . . . Agitation is after all the civilised peaceful weapon of moral force. It is preferable to violence and brute force." Thus, the newspaper proclaimed, "let the African Nationalist agitate."[16] Likewise, as the pages of the *Evening News* aimed to spread the message of African self-determination and popular mobilization in the Gold Coast, Nkrumah and those allied with him in the UGCC formed their own radical wing within the organization, the Committee on Youth Organisations (CYO). Over the next ten months, the CYO would operate what historian Richard Rathbone has described as a "party within a party." The CYO would in turn establish a wide-ranging network of Nkrumah-aligned UGCC branches throughout much of the colony. In addition, it would also operate a system of schools for Gold Coast youth removed from or left out of the colony's educational system.[17]

By mid-1949, however, tensions between the Nkrumah-aligned CYO and the UGCC's broader leadership became unsustainable. In competing meetings in June, the CYO and the Working Committee of the UGCC separately met to discuss their future. On June 11, the Working Committee announced that it was expelling Nkrumah and the CYO from the organization on charges including that "the C. Y. O. is working against the Convention and is determined to break the united front of the country." It also argued that Nkrumah specifically "had undermined the Convention, abused its leaders, and stolen their ideas."[18] A day later in Saltpond, the same town in which the UGCC had been founded nearly two years earlier, Nkrumah announced the inauguration of his own political party, the Convention People's Party (CPP). As the *Evening News* would outline over the ensuing months, the CPP was to be a mass party committed to immediate African self-governance in the Gold Coast. Writing in a July issue of the newspaper, party member Mensa Abrompa outlined the party's mission for the public:

(1) To us has come the great call; we have seen the vision of freedom and we will not rest or turn away till we have achieved our hearts' desire.

(2) We are fighting for our freedom, for the freedom of our country and faith. We desire to injure no nation or people. We wish to have no dominion over others. But we must be perfectly free in our own God-given land and live as free men.

(3) Self-government is our goal; let us have it now to govern or misgovern ourselves.[19]

Moreover, in an editorial that appeared in the same issue of the newspaper, the *Evening News* outlined what it meant to be a member of a mass party like the CPP. According to the newspaper, all Gold Coasters had the responsibility to help bring the CPP's dreams to fruition. "You," the *Evening News* pronounced, "you personally must try to break down that perilous apathy that has taken hold of some members of the community through long years of imperialist domination." Most importantly, this responsibility included helping to enroll new members in the party, further expanding the party's reach into all of the colony's many different communities.[20]

As the CPP sought to expand its influence throughout the Gold Coast, Nkrumah personally sought to position himself as the voice of the Gold Coast anticolonial movement. Much as he had sought to do in Great Britain with the WANS, Nkrumah gathered a small inner circle—including individuals like Kojo Botsio, who had worked with him in the WANS—who would help direct the party's mobilization efforts. As 1949 came to a close, the party increasingly sought to have its will felt on the colony-wide political stage as it called for a general strike on January 8, 1950, a day it declared as "Positive Action Day." Structured along the lines of the Gandhian non-violent activism of the 1920s, Positive Action, Nkrumah would explain in a 1949 pamphlet, was a consciousness-raising movement aimed at bringing together the Gold Coast population in an active and collective demand for African self-governance.[21] The colonial state, for its part, responded to the strike by declaring an emergency and arresting Nkrumah and several other key figures in the CPP on charges of sedition and initiating an illegal strike. Shortly thereafter, Nkrumah would be sentenced to three years in prison, further catapulting his popularity. In December 1950, as the Gold Coast government announced dates for the colony's first popularly held elections scheduled for February 1951, Nkrumah sat in prison as the most recognizable figure on the Gold Coast political stage. As a result, when the elections took place in February, the CPP swept the polls, securing thirty-four of the Legislative Assembly's thirty-eight contested seats. In his Accra constituency, Nkrumah himself would receive more than 90 percent of the vote.[22]

* * *

Following the election, crowds rushed to James Fort Prison on Accra's coast, where Nkrumah was being held, to wait for his release. Upon his release on February 12, the crowds ushered Nkrumah to Christiansborg Castle, where he attained the position of leader of government business. A year later, he would gain the title of prime minister, leading a new government in which the African-run Gold Coast Legislative Assembly and the CPP-dominated cabinet gained responsibility for most of the colony's domestic affairs, while the British maintained authority over the colony's foreign affairs. Thus, neither independent nor siloed away from the colony's political decision-making process, Nkrumah and the CPP government he oversaw were positioned in a state of limbo during what would become six years of Afro-Anglo shared governance in the Gold Coast. Critics, including some in the increasingly defunct UGCC and its successor, the Ghana Congress Party, questioned the sincerity of the CPP's founding demands for "self-government now," mocking Nkrumah and the CPP for their failure to achieve full self-governance.[23] Even more disconcerting for the CPP, many of those who ostensibly supported its mission—and who, in many cases, were members of the party itself—had begun to argue that the party had increasingly become beholden to the British as talk of immediate self-government began to fade. As one man explained to the African American writer Richard Wright in 1953, many in the group of which he was a part felt that "the British are using the CPP just as they had used the chiefs." According to Wright, the political realities of CPP rule in the early 1950s had proven a disappointment as, at least for this individual and his colleagues, they "want a more fundamental revolution than what the CPP has brought about."[24]

For Nkrumah, the push and pull of the enthusiasm on the occasion of his release from James Fort Prison and the pressures of dissent and disappointment coming from both the official opposition and segments of the general population would mark the fifteen years he would serve as prime minister and, from 1960, president of the Gold Coast and then Ghana. The challenge for Nkrumah was that of balancing his own political vision for the emergent country and Africa as a whole with the realities on the ground in the Gold Coast/Ghana and the postwar international community more broadly. Nkrumah's experiences in the United States and Great Britain had instilled in him a fundamentally pan-African view of the challenges facing the country he governed. As Nkrumah would suggest in his published works and speeches throughout his career, as a colony the Gold Coast, like its neighbors, found itself beholden to a European colonial system rooted in the unalloyed extraction of its resources for European political and economic gain. The remedy to any colony's exploitation was at once political and economic, Nkrumah would contend throughout the 1950s and 1960s and had outlined as early as 1947 in *Towards Colonial Freedom.* Complete and unconditional political independence must be the first and most fundamental step in the liberation process, for, he would assert, no new country—let alone colony—could construct an economic system that was built to serve the needs and wishes of its own people under the guise of colonial rule. The pull of imperial exploitation was simply too strong.

As Nkrumah would also outline throughout his career, imperialism should not be seen only as a mechanism of territorial control. At its core, he would argue, it was the root of the global capitalist system and stood at the foundation of the twentieth-century international order. As a result, it not only created the political world in which colonized peoples lived, it also fundamentally shaped the ways in which colonized peoples interacted with one another as well as how they and colonizing peoples related to one another. It altered everything from the religions to which people adhered to what they bought and where they shopped, to the languages they spoke and much more. Imperialism, for Nkrumah, was in essence a force that continuously found new ways to reach further into the depths of not just those of the colonized but everyone's lives—political, social, cultural, and economic—for it had sculpted the rules, expectations, and perceived possibilities of the modern world. The consequence in many communities, Nkrumah and others would lament, was a binding of colonized peoples to a colonial mentality that inextricably connected them to their colonial pasts even after independence. The goal of independence, then, was not just political self-determination, but personal and social reinvention. Speaking to a group of trade unionists in 1960 at the opening of the Hall of Trade Unions, Nkrumah emphasized both the possibilities of this process of re-invention and the continued threat of imperialism to newly independent states like Ghana. "The fundamental conviction which we have derived from our cruel colonial past," Nkrumah advised the trade unionists, "is that Africa can no longer trust in anybody except herself and her resources. . . . Imperialism, having been forced out through the door of modern African nationalism, may yet attempt to return through the window, and the workers must be on their guard. The world must realize that there is today a new African who is determined to challenge the entrenched positions of the old order and to build a new Africa where he is master of himself."[25]

As such, Nkrumah tended to understand the challenges facing the Gold Coast/Ghana in terms much more expansive than the national boundaries of the emergent state would suggest. In other words, the issues facing the Gold Coast/Ghana could not be addressed in isolation; they were part of an international system of colonial exploitation that was global in nature, not national. It was a system, he would argue, that could only be subverted through a concerted and united effort of colonized peoples to create an alternative. As early as 1953, Nkrumah and the CPP began to lay the groundwork for transforming the Gold Coast into the African epicenter of such a transnational movement of anticolonial activism. In December, the CPP held its first pan-African conference as a party in political power in the colony's famed second city, Kumasi—the capital of the historic Asante empire. Ama Biney presents the conference as "Nkrumah's brainchild," arguing that he and the conference's other organizers viewed the event as a continuation of the anticolonial pan-Africanism articulated in Manchester, albeit with a strategic focus on West Africa.[26] Included among the event's participants were Nnamdi Azikiwe and George Padmore, who, despite his Caribbean origins, represented Liberia. Coming out of the meeting, the conference delegates announced, was a desire to form a "strong and truly federal state [in West Africa], capable of protecting itself from outside invasion and able to preserve its internal security."[27] The congress's delegates further argued that the new federal state was to be rooted in a blending of the principles of parliamentary democracy with a respect for "the traditions of the various communities" that comprised it. As described in a 1954 issue of the *West African Review*, the new federation was also to have a broader pan-African mission to "cultivate friendship of States interested in the destiny of Africa and identify itself with the Commonwealth of Nations."[28]

In comparison to earlier pan-African conferences to which its organizers saw this one as a successor, the Kumasi congress was a relatively small affair, with approximately twenty official delegates in attendance.[29] Nkrumah's and the CPP's pan-African ambitions, however, only grew through the 1950s and independence in March 1957 provided a new opening for Nkrumah and the Ghanaian government he oversaw to build the global and continental anticolonial movement he envisioned. As a result, approximately a month after independence, Nkrumah announced his intention to host leaders from each of Africa's nine independent states in Accra for the first Conference of Independent African States (CIAS). Initially scheduled for October 1957, the conference would take place in April of the following year, bringing together leaders and prominent officials from eight of the continent's independent states, with only South Africa's apartheid government refusing to participate absent invitations to the colonial powers.[30] As envisaged by Nkrumah, the CIAS was to be an opportunity for the continent's leaders to not only build diplomatic linkages, but to also begin the process of reimagining Africa's place in the international community.

As planning for the event took shape over the course of 1957, personal and diplomatic rivalries forced a narrowing of the conference's goals so as to ensure full participation.[31] Regardless, Nkrumah opened the event on April 15, 1958, by advocating for a new, united Africa driven by what he described as an "African Personality" manifested in the continent's shared history of both struggle and connection. He outlined a history of Afro-European interactions in Africa scaffolded by the successive violence of the European slave trade into the Atlantic and the subsequent Scramble for Africa in the nineteenth century. He similarly denounced the white supremacy underlying the colonial project as a whole before presenting the African Personality as an affirmative expression of Africans' "individual and collective interests." As outlined by Nkrumah, these interests were foremost to be expressed in a peaceful struggle for the right to African self-determination.[32] A week later, as the conference came to a close, Nkrumah again returned to the idea of the African Personality and of Africa itself as he denounced the racialized colonial language that featured prominently in popular understandings of the continent. This language included referring to an "Arab Africa" and a "Black Africa," an "Islamic Africa" and a "Non-Islamic" Africa, and a "Mediterranean Africa" and a "Tropical Africa." "We [as Africans] are one," Nkrumah firmly declared. It was thus within the unity of the African Personality, he continued, that Africans "in the future . . . [will] play *a positive role* and speak with a concerted voice in the cause of Peace, and for the liberation of dependent Africa and in defence of our national independence, sovereignty, and territorial integrity."[33]

Almost immediately following the close of the CIAS in April 1958, Nkrumah and the CPP hosted another, much larger pan-African conference in Accra in December 1958. Featuring more than two hundred delegates from political parties and anticolonial movements from throughout the continent, the first All-African People's Conference (AAPC) distinguished itself from the CIAS, which was fundamentally a diplomatic event, by being designed as an extragovernmental affair aimed at opening a much more expansive dialogue around questions of African self-determination, anticolonial mobilization, and African unity. As Nkrumah would describe at the event's opening, the AAPC was the first event of its kind on the continent, paving the way for a diverse collection "of African Freedom Fighters not only to come together, but to assemble in a free independent African State for the purpose of planning for a final assault upon Imperialism and Colonialism."[34] Coinciding with the conference was the promise of a £10 million Ghanaian aid package to the newly independent West African state of Guinea, which the French sought to punish for its no vote in the 1958 referendum on joining the newly created French Community with an immediate and unstructured independence.[35] Coming out of the aid package was a broader agreement between Nkrumah and the Guinean president Sékou Touré for a union between the two countries that was to serve as an experiment in pan-African, extraterritorial sovereignty, as each state ceded a portion of its sovereignty to the newly formed supraterritorial union. By 1960, Mali would join, with Nkrumah also claiming that a similar union between Ghana and the Congo had also been agreed upon prior to Congolese prime minister Patrice Lumumba's 1960 arrest.[36]

In the ensuing years, Nkrumah's pan-Africanism took many different forms as he sought to use both the Ghanaian state and the CPP party apparatus to advance the cause of African liberation and unity on the continent and beyond. These efforts included holding additional pan-African conferences and meetings—both at the governmental and extragovernmental levels—within the country during the early 1960s. Moreover, it also included establishing Accra and Ghana more broadly as the sites for a burgeoning community of anticolonial activists, pan-Africanists, and freedom fighters during Ghana's first decade of self-rule. Among those who made their way to Nkrumah's Ghana during the period were George Padmore, who served as Nkrumah's advisor on African affairs, Malcolm X, Frantz Fanon, Patrice Lumumba, W. E. B. Du Bois, Shirley Graham Du Bois, Maya Angelou, Robert Mugabe, and Félix Moumié, among many others. Additionally, Nkrumah also established an elaborate bureaucratic infrastructure within the Ghanaian state designed to house, educate, and cater to the needs of Ghana's growing expatriate and activist community as well as to shepherd their activism toward the pan-African interests and ambitions of the Ghanaian state itself.[37]

For continental and diasporic Africans alike, Nkrumah's and the Ghanaian government's efforts in cultivating this pan-African community within the still young country offered a sense of both hope and opportunity as they pursued their own anticolonial ambitions. As one recent African American arrival to Ghana explained to a group gathered at Maya Angelou's Accra house in the early 1960s, he and his partner had come to Ghana "because of Nkrumah"; they hoped to be nourished, he asserted, by the transformations taking place in the country and continent.[38] Likewise, writing to Nkrumah in 1960, Adelino Chitofo Guambe—a young Mozambican activist living in Southern Rhodesia (Zimbabwe)—praised his pan-African ambitions for the continent. "Dr. Nkrumah," Guambe asserted, "with his politics and ideas is [the] true son of Africa," before the Mozambican transitioned to asking the Ghanaian president for financial support so he could make his way to Ghana. As he continued, Guambe explained that he "wish[ed] to learn more about politics, but," he noted, "without money I can not [sic], I only expect a great help from you true (MESSIAH) of Africa. . . . I know I shall learn too much from you and others in Ghana, I feel all my will power to force me but only monetary problems are stopping me."[39]

Letters such as Guambe's to Nkrumah and various other branches of the Ghanaian government were not unique during the early 1960s. A year earlier, Ntsu Mokhehle—the leader of the Basutoland Congress Party and member of the AAPC Steering Committee—also wrote to Nkrumah requesting support from the Ghanaian president and his government. "My country is completely surrounded by the Union of South Africa," Mokhehle reminded Nkrumah. "We feel we are so placed that if we could be helped and strengthened to independence, we would be very useful to the A. A. P. C. in breaking down the apartheid policy of the Union of South Africa by running a democratic state within the borders of the Union." As a result, Mokhehle requested assistance in establishing a weekly newspaper, obtaining a printing press, three jeeps, and "scholarships to enable our boys and girls to study in Ghana where the atmosphere of freedom would open their eyes."[40] Likewise, in 1960, E. T. Makiwane—a South African teacher living in western Nigeria—similarly requested assistance from the All-African Trade Union Federation to help his brother, "who has escaped from South Africa to Basutoland [Lesotho]," make his way to Bechuanaland (Botswana). According to Makiwane, he was soliciting Nkrumah's and Ghana's support for this endeavor because, unlike his adopted home of Nigeria, which was "a mere colony," "Ghana has taken the lead in rendering help . . . and I am particularly grateful to the Ghana Government for such a progressive step."[41]

* * *

For Nkrumah and the various offices within and affiliated with the Ghanaian government that received letters asking for assistance from throughout the continent, the letters represented what Nkrumah and the CPP interpreted as widespread popular support for Nkrumah's pan-African vision for the continent. To Nkrumah, who, as noted in chapter 2, famously marked Ghana's 1957 independence with the declaration that Ghana's "independence is meaningless unless it is linked up with the total liberation of the African continent," cultivating a transnational constituency for his vision for the continent was not simply for show.[42] It was foundational to his reading of the postwar world. If colonialism had created the territorial boundaries that marked the African map, Nkrumah surmised, it was surely in the interests of the imperial powers to sustain these artificial divisions during the decolonization process so as to sustain their continued exploitation of the continent's peoples and resources. The rise of the Cold War only further proved to Nkrumah the necessity of such a transnational constituency, for the diplomatic struggle between the United States and the Soviet Union sought to force the world's ever-growing number of new nation-states to align themselves—politically, economically, and, in some cases, even socially and culturally—with one or the other of the world's superpowers. A strong and united Africa, Nkrumah would thus argue throughout his tenure in office, did not simply promise Africa a voice on the international stage. It was necessary in order to assure it a voice that would be listened to. Speaking to the Ghanaian National Assembly in 1963 on the establishment of the Organization of African Unity, Nkrumah reminded his Ghanaian colleagues, as he had done many times in his career, that "with our continental liberation and unity, Africa will become a powerful force that will carry its total impact in the councils of the world."[43]

5

Between Nation and Pan-Africanism

Part II

By the 1963 formation of the Organization of African Unity, Kwame Nkrumah had long established himself as the preeminent voice on the question of African liberation and unity on the African continent and had simultaneously positioned Ghana at the epicenter of the global pan-African movement. As Nkrumah did so, however, events on the continent would also come to challenge the implementation of the Ghanaian president's vision of an independent and united Africa, leading him to increasingly radicalize his interpretation of the politics and praxis of decolonization. For Nkrumah in the early 1960s, no event shook his view of the decolonization process more than the 1961 assassination of the Congolese prime minister Patrice Lumumba, coming just months after Nkrumah had committed more than two thousand Ghanaian peacekeeping troops to the newly independent Congo.[1] Arriving as part of a broader United Nations peacekeeping mission, Ghana's troops in the Congo were there primarily, to Nkrumah's mind, with the mission of helping to protect Lumumba's democratically elected government. Additional challenges such as the persisting settler colonialism found in North Africa, southern Africa, and the Portuguese colonies only further undermined Nkrumah's faith in what had previously been a cornerstone of his political philosophy—the necessity of nonviolent anticolonial resistance in the struggle for African independence. Not only would his government come to fund and train expatriate freedom fighters within Ghana, it would also recruit and train Ghanaians to join in anticolonial struggles in other parts of the continent.[2] By the end of the 1960s, Nkrumah himself would begin theorizing the virtues of armed struggle in anticolonial liberation.

Further challenging Nkrumah's vision for the continent were the many disparate visions for Africa's future coming out of the continent's ever-increasing number of independent states during the late 1950s and early 1960s. As noted in chapter 4, Guinea joined the still small community of independent African states in late 1958 following its October independence. Over the next two years, the number of newly independent African states would increase rapidly, with seventeen countries achieving their independence in 1960 alone. These newly independent figures on the African political stage included all of French West and Equatorial Africa, the Democratic Republic of the Congo, Nigeria, and Somalia. Many of the leaders and governments of these new states came to question Nkrumah's methods and agenda for the continent, while others would even come to question Nkrumah's prominence as a leader on the international stage.[3] Likewise, members of the expatriate and freedom-fighter communities in Accra at times also wrote to Nkrumah and others within the Ghanaian government to express their disappointment with everything from their accommodations and employment opportunities to the progress of the Nkrumah administration in fulfilling the promises of Nkrumah's anticolonial vision. Writing to Nkrumah, for instance, in May 1960, Bakary Djibo—the leader of Niger's exiled Sawaba party—complained that he and Sawaba had not received the cooperation they had anticipated from the Ghanaian government following their arrival in Accra. Nkrumah, for his part, replied to Djibo promising his government's full support to the Nigerien party, while simultaneously insisting that "this does depend upon SAWABA's trained and competent people being here to see that the organisation is carried out as well as possible."[4]

Inside Ghana, Kwame Nkrumah's pan-African ambitions and activities not only shaped his and his Convention People's Party (CPP) government's domestic agenda but, more fundamentally, buttressed the way he understood the potential of Ghana itself and how Ghanaians viewed him and his government. As Nkrumah came to power in the early 1950s, he outlined an ambitious political, social, economic, and cultural program for the country, one in which he sought to transform nearly every facet of Ghanaian daily life. Focusing on social groups often distanced from the circles of power within both precolonial and colonial social structures—women, workers, the unemployed, and youth—Nkrumah argued that the potential of the continent's people had been stunted by the social structures underpinning both colonial rule and many aspects of African traditional society. Distinct, often hereditarily and generationally bounded hierarchies, he and the CPP would suggest, did not merely consolidate power in the hands of a few. More broadly, they also suppressed innovation within African communities as they reinforced power structures and social relationships assumed by Nkrumah and the CPP to be archaic. Colonial rule only further ossified these precolonial hierarchies by prioritizing the voices of chiefs and other elders in both governmental affairs and the distribution of resources within the Gold Coast and similar colonies. The result, Nkrumah emphasized, was a local political and social environment perceived to be backward in relation to the broader modern world and thus more susceptible to colonial exploitation.[5]

* * *

The first decade of Nkrumah's rule in the Gold Coast/ Ghana was marked by a range of political, social, and infrastructural investments designed to restructure key aspects of Ghanaian life. Education proved perhaps the most foundational element of Nkrumah's vision for the Gold Coast/Ghana. As early as 1943, while still in the United States, Nkrumah wrote of the centrality of education to Africa's future, arguing for an educational program for the continent that was in many ways modeled on that which he had received at Achimota in the late 1920s. The goal, as he imagined it, was an educational system designed to "produce a new class of educated Africans imbued with the culture of the west but nevertheless attached to their environment [African heritage]." Tying this vision of African education to his burgeoning ideas of African liberation, Nkrumah went on to add a political dimension to the educational system he envisioned. In doing so, he tied this "new class of Africans" to the advancement of the struggle for African self-determination.[6] Nkrumah continued to hold such views as he joined the United Gold Coast Convention (UGCC) in the late 1940s. By 1949, calls for the extension of African educational opportunities and critiques of the colonial educational system featured prominently in the Nkrumah-founded *Accra Evening News*.[7] When Nkrumah and the CPP came to power in 1951, one of the government's first acts was the creation of a set of measures designed to extend educational opportunities to as many Gold Coasters as possible. By far the most important of these was the inauguration of fee-free primary education in the colony, which was set to go into effect the following year. A decade later, the government would extend fee-free education to middle school students.

As a result, the number of schools and students in the Gold Coast/Ghana skyrocketed over the course of the 1950s and early 1960s. By Ghana's 1957 independence, an additional 350,000 students would join the country's primary and middle schools, compared to the number when Nkrumah came into office in 1951, for a total of more than 570,000 students. The number of primary schools also rose from approximately 1,000 to more than 3,400, with similarly proportioned increases at the middle and secondary school levels.[8] Likewise, a number of curricular reforms undertaken by the Nkrumah government sought to transform the country's teaching and learning practices by moving away from the rote memorization that marked the colonial education program to a pedagogy founded upon experiential learning with a particular focus on the sciences. In doing so, the Nkrumah government invested in teacher training programs, the importation of expatriate teachers, and the development of new labs and acquisition of quality laboratory equipment for schools. In Ghanaian schools, under Nkrumah's "cult of science," as Abena Dove Osseo-Asare describes it, "students ran simple chemical reactions and created science fairs for their parents, successfully raising awareness of the scientific method." As a result, Osseo-Asare concludes that this commitment to scientific education should "be read as a radical call for equality and equity."[9] Moreover, the opening of the sciences to girls and young women in particular stood at the center of the Nkrumah government's scientific educational agenda as it aimed to open new spaces for Ghanaian young women within the Ghanaian public sphere.[10]

Even those who opposed Nkrumah often found it difficult to challenge his government's educational policies. Much of the focus turned to questions of implementation and efficacy. Writing, for instance, in the *Daily Graphic*—the Gold Coast's and later Ghana's most prominent newspaper—the newspaper's editor and Nkrumah's first biographer, Bankole Timothy, chided the Nkrumah government in 1952 for the speed with which the government implemented fee-free primary education in the colony. Specifically, Timothy focused his attention on what he deemed the lack of teacher preparation that accompanied the government's democratization of education. As the Sierra Leonean journalist argued in his reflections on visits to several of the colony's schools, the government was correct in understanding that education should be seen as "the foundation of the development of the Gold Coast." However, he continued, the government had ultimately failed to do the hard work of preparing all involved—teachers, students, parents, and local communities—for the practical challenges embedded in taking on the task of trying to universalize primary education in the colony.[11]

Five years later, S. G. Antor, the leader of the Togoland Congress Party, returned to many of these same themes in the Ghanaian National Assembly as he characterized the Nkrumah government's educational policies as "appalling, deplorable, and disgraceful." Like Timothy, who Nkrumah would deport from Ghana in August 1957, Antor cited a lack of teacher training, while also arguing that times for promotion for students at all levels should be shortened so as to give "the pupils and students the maximum benefit of the educational system in the shortest possible time."[12] Other opposition members continued the assault, complaining of the government's reliance on pupil teachers as opposed to fully trained, professional teachers and a system whereby local governments were asked to finance the schools but had little authority over the running of the schools themselves.[13] Still others objected to the "huge sums of money being spent on education in this country" and to what they perceived to be the uncertain results coming from such an investment. According to United Party (UP) member Jatoe Kaleo, reflecting on the country's schools in 1958, the state of the country's educational system had left him "wondering whether . . . the students who are now being turned out are going to contribute materially to the progress of Ghana." What he claimed to see within the country's schools was at its foundation a system that failed to educate its pupils in the skills they would need to support themselves and advance the country, thus potentially leaving them "roaming the streets of Accra and other big towns . . . disappointed."[14]

Despite the critiques coming from various segments of the press and opposition, for many Ghanaians, the Nkrumah government's educational policies proved one of its most enduring legacies. It was also one that many Ghanaians attributed to Nkrumah specifically. As the prominent Ghanaian historian Kwame Arhin noted in the opening of his short biography of Nkrumah, for people like Arhin's mother, Nkrumah "had immortalized himself" with his belief that *everybody must go to School.*[15] As was the case with Nkrumah's own early education several decades earlier, for both students and parents the opportunity for a child to go to school opened a whole new range of personal, social, and economic prospects. For many, the Nkrumah government's opening up of the country's educational system meant access to careers and jobs that previously would not have been available to them for reasons of class, gender, region, religion, and/or ethnicity. It also held the potential for more favorable marriage prospects due to the sense of social mobility that often came with an education. Likewise, it additionally offered opportunities for wealth and property accumulation and, for a select few, much as was the case for Nkrumah himself, the chance to continue their education abroad. As a result, by the mid-1960s the Nkrumah government had created an educational system that was deeply coveted throughout the continent and one that was educating more than six times the number of students as the colonial government was when Nkrumah came into power more than a decade earlier.[16]

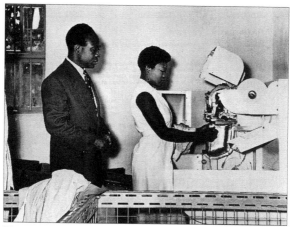

Figure 5.1. Kwame Nkrumah watching machine-label manufacturing, 1957. Photo reproduced courtesy of the United Kingdom's National Archives image library.

Likewise, as the Nkrumah government sought to transform the country's educational system, it simultaneously sought to modernize the infrastructure and productive capabilities of the emergent Ghana. During the first decade of Nkrumah's tenure in office, Accra underwent a massive infrastructural and architectural renovation, with new roads, hospitals, hotels, museums, and community centers coming to dot the city's landscape. Other major cities, most notably including Kumasi, experienced similar makeovers during the period, while even more foundational changes occurred in sites like Tema and Akosombo to the east of Accra. In the cases of both Tema and Akosombo, the government aimed to revolutionize the landscape with the creation of new cities designed to transform the Ghanaian economy from one rooted in export-driven cash-crop agriculture to one founded upon industrial self-sufficiency. In Tema, which prior to 1951 had been a fishing village of approximately four thousand people, Nkrumah and his government imagined a planned city of more than seventy-five thousand people, with some aligned to the government even projecting a population of more than two hundred thousand.[17] At the heart of the new Tema was to be a modern industrial harbor and a range of new industries that would have the potential to produce an ever-growing number of commercial goods for domestic consumption and even export. Such industry, Nkrumah argued, would not only provide new pathways to employment and wealth accumulation for Ghanaian workers, it would also and more fundamentally weaken the former colonial powers and their allies in the West's continued influence over the country by ensuring that the new Ghana was not reliant on Western goods. In short, through places like Tema, Ghanaian resources were to be manufactured by Ghanaian workers in Ghanaian factories for Ghanaian consumers.[18]

The project in Akosombo was even more ambitious. A planned city like Tema, Akosombo was designed to support the construction of a mega-dam across the nearby Volta River and house much of the dam's administration after completion. Stretching from Burkina Faso to Ada on Ghana's Atlantic Coast, the Volta forms the heart of a river system that connects the savannas of northern Ghana and Burkina Faso with the forests of central Ghana and the plains of Ghana's coast. Initial interest in damming the Volta had arisen as far back as the early twentieth century as a British geologist, Sir Albert Kitson, discovered large reserves of bauxite, the ore from which aluminum is produced. Kitson began developing a proposal from which to utilize the hydroelectric power of the river to process the Gold Coast's bauxite reserves. Kitson's discovery and proposal to build a dam initiated a nearly forty-year process in which the colonial government researched the industrial potential of the river, yet never committed to the project. By 1952, Nkrumah's year-old government in Accra released plans for the project that included a dam approximately 1.5 kilometers north of Akosombo, an alumina plant and smelter approximately twenty kilometers south in Kpong, and a railway line connecting Kpong to the yet-to-be-built harbor in Tema.[19]

Over the next decade, the details of the plan would change considerably as Nkrumah and his government negotiated with British and then American stakeholders over questions of financing, politics, and engineering. Eventually, in 1964, Sir Robert Jackson—the Australian head of the Volta River Project (VRP) Preparatory Commission—outlined that the project had three fundamental features: the generation of the Volta's hydroelectric power, the completion of Tema harbor and a modern highway connecting Tema and Akosombo, and a massive smelter in Tema.[20] The damming of the river was also to create what would become one of the world's largest man-made lakes, requiring the resettlement of nearly eighty thousand people. In return for their displacement, the government promised those relocated access to new, modern villages with schools, modern housing, fertile agricultural land, and mechanized farming.[21]

The VRP was to serve as the cornerstone of Nkrumah's industrial vision for Ghana and West Africa. The bauxite mined and processed as a result of the project was envisioned as catapulting Ghana into an industrial power by helping to finance other industries, while also providing the country with the ability to transform itself into a major player in the global market of a commodity utilized for everything from clothing to building materials.[22] Even more fundamentally, the project was to provide the electrical power for nearly all of Nkrumah's industrial and economic plans for the country. As with elsewhere in the world, electricity was both a practical necessity for an industrializing country in the twentieth century and a political and cultural symbol of the country's modernization. This reality did not escape Nkrumah and his government as they sought to celebrate the VRP both domestically and internationally. As a result, the government prominently featured the project in an elaborate parade of roadshows, exhibits, films, pamphlets, and other media, all aimed at presenting the VRP as the keystone of an independent and modern Ghana.[23] As one former official of the Nkrumah administration's

Ministry of Finance, Kwame Kwarteng, reminisced in a 1992 BBC documentary, for Nkrumah, the potential and benefits of the dam project were limitless. "At one stage," Kwarteng, who was a member of the team involved in negotiating the dam project, explained, "he [Nkrumah] said he wanted the project to light up every hamlet in this country, and at the same time as a by-product, to have an irrigation project which will transform the whole of the Accra Plains into a granary."[24]

* * *

By the early 1960s, Nkrumah and his government had begun to facilitate a radical reenvisioning of the possibilities of Ghanaian political, social, and economic life. For Nkrumah in particular, none of these changes could or should be read as solely Ghanaian, however. Even the most seemingly domestic of projects, such as the government's investments in the country's educational system and social services, not only had pan-African implications, but, in many cases, were explicitly designed to serve as models or catalysts for imagined, larger reinventions of the broader African political, social, and economic scene. Writing in 1957, Richard Wright described the changes taking place in Ghana as "a kind of pilot project of the new Africa." For Wright, the question that therefore stood at the center of the Nkrumahist project in Ghana and Africa was the dialectical relationship between the "modern" and the "traditional" in the

127

new society Nkrumah envisioned. As such, it was the unknown potential of this synthesis that made Nkrumah and his political imaginings so exciting, complex, and uncertain.[25]

Inside Ghana, the day-to-day aspects of the changes Nkrumah sought to bring to Ghanaian life often met with mixed reactions. As noted, his democratization of the country's educational system, especially at the primary level, elicited widespread praise throughout much of the country, as did investments in such projects as the extension of the country's road networks, youth employment programs, and various other social services. Larger-scale projects such as the resettlement programs associated with the VRP and the construction of Tema harbor tended to enjoy more qualified support and even opposition, especially among those most directly affected by the schemes. In each case, the government's actions garnered regular complaints and even protests from the displaced about broken promises, inadequate accommodations and economic opportunities in their new communities, and disconnection from their ancestral lands.[26] In other instances, Ghanaians noted with frustration the government's acquisition of families' and communities' farmlands for state farms that in theory were to become emblems of modern, mechanized agriculture in the country, but in practice often resulted in more conventional forms of manual labor.[27] Meanwhile, others complained of what they viewed as the diversion of Ghanaian resources to other African countries as part of Nkrumah's broader pan-African ambitions.[28]

As it sought to do with key aspects of Nkrumah's educational policy, the opposition grabbed hold of the various shortcomings that plagued the implementation of many Nkrumah-era government projects in its critiques of the government's agenda for the country. In the National Assembly in particular, numerous opposition members of Parliament (MPs) questioned the efficacy and even logic of many of the Nkrumah government's projects, most notably including the VRP and Tema. As early as 1954, for instance, J. B. Danquah—speaking in the preindependence Legislative Assembly—turned his attention to the question of financing. As Danquah would argue, much was to be appreciated about the ambitions illustrated in the Volta and Tema projects. However, he insisted that an even braver and more sustainable position in the pursuit of the projects' development aims would have been to ensure that they were undertaken in a manner prioritizing self-sufficiency. According to Danquah, it was only via such a quest for self-sufficiency that even larger issues such as "our incessant request for independence" could be recognized.[29]

Seven years later, UP MP Abayifaa Karbo echoed Danquah's critiques of the Nkrumah government's development agenda in his own address to the National Assembly. Responding to Nkrumah's recent unveiling of the VRP's "Master Agreement," Karbo began like Danquah by congratulating the government for its boldness in proposing the VRP before turning to the vulnerabilities that he saw in the agreement. Eventually signed a year later by Nkrumah to finance the project through a set of loans from the American aluminum firm Kaiser Industries, the master plan required that the government cede authority over key aspects of the project, including the right to use Ghanaian bauxite in the envisioned aluminum smelter and the cost of electricity.[30] For Karbo, commenting on the government's negotiating strategy, Nkrumah's actions in the negotiations were emblematic of a broader trend within Nkrumah's Ghana in which the government would consistently propose new and ever-more-expensive projects that would ultimately contribute little to the country beyond their expense. Alluding to the Builders Brigade—a youth employment project unveiled in 1957—Karbo complained of idleness in the program's workforce as brigaders collected their wages with few accomplishments to show for them. Karbo also highlighted issues with the country's water supply and food shortages he attributed to urban migration away from rural farms. Even more significantly, when he turned to the master agreement itself, Karbo accused Nkrumah and his government of sacrificing key features of Ghana's hard-fought sovereignty in pursuit of the dam project.[31]

Nkrumah and his government responded to such accusations with frustration and, at times, even contempt. In parliamentary debates, Nkrumah's allies regularly came to the president's defense as they cast the opposition's critiques of the government and of Nkrumah himself as petty and without merit. Responding to Karbo specifically, K. A. Gbedemah—then minister of finance—dismissed the MP's concerns as out of hand and off point before a parade of CPP-aligned MPs personalized the debate around the VRP as one tied to Nkrumah himself.[32] Grace Ayensu, holder of one of the prescribed women's seats in the parliament, insisted that, with the signing of the master agreement, "Osagyefo's [Nkrumah's] dream has now come true. With Osagyefo's wisdom and foresight, Ghana's Volta River Project is going to be started."[33] Likewise, John Arjarquah of the Mid-Volta district talked of the anticipated widespread employment benefits the project would bring to the country, along with the splendor of the new township and hydroelectricity that would follow. "Evidently," he opined, "the Osagyefo and his Government have struggled and are still struggling for our betterment, prosperity, happiness, and for everything that goes to make life worth living." Arjarquah then proceeded to call upon all of his colleagues to "in the name of the whole nation . . . thank the Osagyefo and his Government for this marvelous and noble achievement."[34]

Similar patterns followed both opposition critiques of the government's policies and development efforts through the early 1960s and the CPP's response to them. However, in the case of both those who supported and those who challenged the government, reflections on the Nkrumah government and its agenda regularly morphed into personalized commentaries on Nkrumah himself. Inside the CPP and particularly in its press, Nkrumah had long been exalted as the party's visionary and largely unquestioned leader. As early as the late 1940s, the *Evening News* had led the charge in celebrating Nkrumah in the press by presenting the Ghanaian president as the "Apostle to Ghana Youth" and his as the "name [to which] every head should bow . . . for what he is trying to do as a citizen of Ghanaland."[35] The celebration of Nkrumah would continue throughout the 1950s, with the party and its press almost invariably presenting its accomplishments as inextricably linked to the actions and ideas of Nkrumah himself. By the early 1960s, however, such celebrations would intensify even further as popular slogans such as "Nkrumah Never Dies" gained an ever-growing currency in party circles, while many prominent officials openly compared Nkrumah to the Messiah.[36] Similarly, supporters regularly attributed to Nkrumah such titles as *katakyie* ("the intrepid"), *kasapreko* ("the one who could not be contradicted"), and *oburoni suro* ("the white man fears him").[37]

To those in the opposition, the CPP's increasing and what they perceived as its over-the-top elevation of Nkrumah exemplified what opposition officials consistently portrayed as Nkrumah's and the CPP's antidemocratic practices. As with the CPP's discourse, Nkrumah himself stood in as the embodiment of the government and its agenda in the opposition commentary. Accusations of authoritarianism had haunted Nkrumah from the earliest years of his tenure in office as opposition MPs and the newspapers aligned to them regularly presented him as an aspiring dictator who aimed to quell all voices of dissent within the emergent country.[38] Others portrayed him and his agenda as un-Ghanaian and un-African. At the heart of many of these attacks were deeply personal questions over Nkrumah's family history, origin, and, prior to his 1957 marriage, his bachelorhood. Speaking, for instance, in 1956 in the southeastern Gold Coast town of Anloga, Nancy Tsiboe—an activist in the Asante-based National Liberation Movement—insisted to her audience that they would "all agree . . . that only a married man with a family knows how to manage a home." Tsiboe went on to maintain that it would only make sense that "he [a married man] can manage a country." Lacking a wife, legitimate children, and supposedly coming from a genealogical line with potentially non–Gold Coast roots, Nkrumah, Tsiboe suggested, was at his core a rootless and illegitimate leader. It was this lack of connection, she argued, that made him predisposed to attack Gold Coast/Ghanaian tradition.[39]

As the government further consolidated its power in the years following independence, the opposition intensified its critiques of Nkrumah, his government's policies, and the narrative surrounding the Ghanaian president. In 1957, as the National Assembly debated the establishment of the Builders Brigade—with its various labor camps for unemployed youth—opposition officials compared the camps to those of Adolph Hitler's Germany. Upon visiting the camps in subsequent years, others insisted that camp life entailed little more than the celebration of Nkrumah himself.[40] Further criticisms of the government emerged as the Nkrumah administration considered the 1958 introduction of preventative detention in the country. As outlined by Nkrumah, preventative detention—the detaining without trial of those deemed threats to the state for up to five years—was a necessary protective measure designed to ensure the security of the state and its national and pan-African agenda. To the opposition, however, the measure represented a clear threat to the legitimacy of the parliamentary democracy established at independence and the personal security of many within its own ranks. Speaking to the National Assembly in July 1958, R. R. Amponsah—a UP MP who in the CPP's earliest days had been one of the party's most prominent Asante members—chided Nkrumah and his government for what he perceived as Ghana's descent into despotism and accused the government of "misusing parliamentary institutions in order to set up a one-party dictatorship in this country."[41]

By the end of 1958, Amponsah himself would be detained, along with fellow UP MP Modesto Apaloo, under the authority of the newly enacted Preventative Detention Act. Amponsah and Apaloo would spend the remainder of Nkrumah's term in office in prison after being accused of working with then Army major

Benjamin Awhaitey to assassinate Nkrumah.[42] Over the next several years, nearly all major figures in what by 1962 would become the defunct UP would find themselves in preventative detention or in exile abroad, along with many prominent former CPP officials who had fallen out of favor with Nkrumah as well as ordinary citizens who had raised the ire of CPP officials at the local or national levels. Writing to Nkrumah from Nsawam Prison in 1964, J. B. Danquah—who spent two stints under preventative detention—described life in prison to his former colleague while also reminding Nkrumah of their own shared 1948 detainment. "I am tired of being in prison on preventative detention with no opportunity to make an original or any contribution to the progress and development of the country," Danquah wrote, asking for his release. "You will recall that when in 1948 we were arrested by the British Government and sent to the North for detention they treated us as gentlemen, and not as galley slaves, and provided each of us with a furnished bungalow (two or three rooms) with a garden, together with opportunity for reading and writing." However, at Nsawam, Danquah continued,

> I find myself locked up . . . in a cell of about six by nine feet, without a writing or reading desk, without a dining table, without a bed, or a chair or any form of seat, and compelled to eat my food squatting on the same floor where two blankets and a cover are spread for me on the hard

cement to sleep on, and where a latrine pan (piss pot) without a closet, and a water jug and a cup without a locker, are all assembled in that narrow space for my use like a galley slave.[43]

Danquah's pleas fell on deaf ears. Over the course of the next seven months, Danquah would become increasingly ill. He would die in prison on February 4, 1965.

* * *

Kwame Nkrumah would govern Ghana for just over one more year after Danquah's death. Much had changed within Ghana in the eighteen years since Danquah's now long-defunct UGCC had invited Nkrumah to return to the Gold Coast and become the organization's general secretary. At the governmental level, by as early as 1960, Nkrumah and the CPP had already begun openly questioning the legitimacy of the political system it adopted at independence as they began to theorize about the necessity and possibilities of a one-party state in Ghana. As outlined by the party press, the parliamentary democracy Ghana adopted in 1957 was simply not conducive to the realities of life and politics in a newly independent state, for it ultimately relied on the actions of what the government classified as a "responsible opposition." The CPP's definition of a responsible opposition was often very slippery and inconsistently applied. Yet from the CPP's perspective, any other sort of opposition ultimately posed a threat to the state as it provided an opening for neocolonial and other anti-state actors to infect the government. The result, it was argued, was a corruption and subversion of the revolutionary agenda envisioned by leaders like Nkrumah. The transition to a one-party state was thus to bring about what the CPP portrayed as a more organic, productive, inclusive, and democratic government built upon a closer relationship between the people and the state.[44] Preventative detention was thus intended to protect the government and its vision for the country from such infiltration by shielding it from what Ghana's first attorney general, Geoffrey Bing, described as "political crime."[45]

By 1964, Nkrumah would call a referendum initiating the formal transformation of the Ghanaian state to a one-party system. Taking place in February, the vote resulted in an implausible landslide in favor of the alteration of the country's constitution, with 92.8 percent of Ghanaians supposedly voting for the one-party state.[46] Party officials would subsequently congratulate themselves for such an impressive showing at the polls, while thanking their colleagues and subordinates for their work and "co-operation . . . [in serving] our illustrious leader, osagyefo dr. kwame nkrumah [sic] at all times."[47] Meanwhile, on the ground, Nkrumah oversaw a popular political context in which nearly all forms of dissent had now been both formally and informally made illegal. The result was a forced silence in the Ghanaian public sphere as many Ghanaians worried that any discussion of politics outside of the strictures defined by the state could potentially result in their detention. Fears of spies abounded, even inside families. By the mid-1960s, prominent institutions that had long had a history of independence in the Gold Coast, such as the Trades Union Congress and the country's various women's organizations, had become inextricably integrated into the CPP or state apparatus. Many also had their missions altered so as to align with the goals and ambitions of the party and state, and their leaders handpicked by—in some cases—Nkrumah himself. What this process of centralization meant for much of their membership was a further silencing of their voices on both the local and national stages. Others, meanwhile, adopted a highly choreographed discourse of their own, celebrating Nkrumah and his vision for Ghana and Africa as they embarked upon an often perilous engagement with the state in the pursuit of their own interests.[48]

6

Exile and an Era of Reinvention

In early 1966, Ho Chi Minh—enmeshed in an intensi-
fying war with the United States in Vietnam—invited
Kwame Nkrumah to the North Vietnamese capital of
Hanoi, purportedly to help mediate the Vietnamese-
American conflict. Despite warnings from a number
of allies around him that he should not leave Ghana
at this time, Nkrumah flew to Hanoi on February 21,
1966. While he was in transit on the morning of February 24, segments of the Ghanaian army and police
attacked key government installations and sites around
Accra, initiating a coup against the longtime Ghanaian president. Nkrumah learned of the coup during a
stopover in China. Meanwhile, inside Ghana, key figures within the Convention People's Party (CPP) now
found themselves hunted by the military and police,
resulting in the arrest of several prominent government and party officials. Others fled the country. The
new military government—calling itself the National
Liberation Council (NLC)—also turned its attention to

Ghana's highly visible expatriate and freedom-fighter community, quickly disbanding it. Most of the community ultimately left the country—some by force, some on their own accord. Furthermore, throughout Ghana, rank-and-file CPP supporters and those perceived to be such, along with members of the party's and state's various wings, faced regular harassment from the police for months after the coup, with many arrested and held for undefined periods. Others, including school-age youth, endured frequent questioning and abuse following the coup.[1]

For Nkrumah's family, the day of the coup brought the battle for Ghana's future to the family's doorstep. Asleep inside the presidential home at Flagstaff House in Accra, as described by Gamal Nkrumah, the then seven-year-old eldest son of Nkrumah's marriage to Fathia (Rizk) Nkrumah, Nkrumah's family was awakened by the "din of artillery fire and explosions" outside. Further adding to the family's and particularly the three Nkrumah children's fear at the time, Gamal Nkrumah explained, was the "roaring of the unfed lions in Accra's zoo, a short distance from Flagstaff House."[2]

Inside the presidential home, Fathia Nkrumah—an Egyptian Copt who nearly a decade earlier had married Nkrumah without having previously met him and without sharing a language—quickly responded to the events outside by telephoning the Egyptian embassy in Accra, connecting just before Flagstaff House's telephone lines were cut. The embassy assured her that it would send a plane to evacuate her and her family from Ghana. As the family awaited the plane, Ghanaian soldiers breached the gates of Flagstaff House, forcing the family to flee. "Everyone," writes Gamal Nkrumah, "Grandmother Nyaneba [Kwame Nkrumah's mother] included, was quickly evacuated and the hostile forces trooped in, ransacking the premises. Mother took a few personal belongings, which were promptly confiscated at a roadside checkpoint. . . . Even family photographs, letters, and souvenirs were taken away." The soldiers then initially took the family to the Egyptian embassy before heading to the police headquarters for questioning. "At gun point," he recalled, "we were ordered out of the car and told to sit on the ground in a clearing in the bush." After waiting for the soldiers—who were radioing back and forth with one another—to decide what to do, the family eventually made their way to the airport. Neither Nkrumah's wife nor his three children would see her husband and their father alive again.[3]

In China, Nkrumah had to decide quickly how to proceed. As he would describe in his 1968 account of the coup, *Dark Days in Ghana,* Nkrumah's initial impulse was to turn around and return to Accra immediately. However, this was not possible, for during a stopover in Burma (Myanmar), the entourage had left its Ghana Airways plane in the capital, Rangoon (Yangon), in favor of Chinese state transport to Peking (Beijing). The result was a multiday delay in Peking as Nkrumah awaited transport. As a result, in his stead, Nkrumah released a statement to the press promising his quick return to the country and encouraging "everyone [in Ghana] at this hour of trial . . . to remain calm, but firm in determination and resistance."[4] Adding to the difficulty of Nkrumah's position in China was the reaction of many of the government and party officials who accompanied him to the news of the coup. Unlike his interpretation of the reactions of the security forces and his personal secretariat, who he presented as stoic in the face of the news, Nkrumah explained in *Dark Days* that many of the politicians with him were far from resolute. Rather, he portrayed them as nervous, anxious, and fearful about what the coup meant for them personally upon their return to Ghana. Several of these officials would eventually abscond back to Ghana in subsequent days in the hope of seeking reconciliation with the new military government. Others would flee into exile. Nearly all, Nkrumah disparagingly complained, had comported themselves not as men, but as "old women."[5]

Kwame Nkrumah would remain in Peking until February 28, when the Soviet Union sent a plane to transport him to Moscow via Irkutsk. From Moscow, Nkrumah would eventually travel to Guinea, where he had been offered refuge, arriving there on March 1, 1966. In *Dark Days,* Nkrumah outlined the reasoning underpinning his decision to travel to Guinea despite offerings of refuge from several other African countries, including Mali and Tanzania. Logistically, the geographic proximity between Guinea and Ghana made it particularly appealing. From the Guinean capital of Conakry, Nkrumah would not only be able to keep abreast of the events in Ghana, but he also could relatively easily hold audiences with Ghanaians traveling to meet him—many of whom, he claimed, made the journey on foot. Additionally, the political relationship between Nkrumah and Guinea's president, Sékou Touré, dated back to 1958, when Nkrumah's government helped bail out the newly independent Guinean state following the latter's impromptu independence. Ghana's and Guinea's relationship was further solidified shortly thereafter with the formation of the Ghana-Guinea Union. Despite failing to materialize into what Nkrumah had imagined for the union, over the next several years Ghana and Guinea would continue to maintain a unique political relationship, which for a time even included the exchange of cabinet-level ministers in each other's government. Upon his arrival in Conakry, Nkrumah was accorded a hero's welcome, replete with the slaughter of nineteen cattle. Even more importantly, in his public address at the event, Sékou Touré announced to the crowd welcoming Nkrumah that, while in Guinea, Nkrumah would serve as the country's president. Nkrumah eventually agreed to copresident.[6]

* * *

Touré initially housed Nkrumah and his entourage in a government compound near the Conakry city center before moving the Ghanaian contingent of more than seventy to a large seaside compound known as Villa Syli, where Nkrumah would reside for the next five years. Nkrumah regularly received news of the events taking place in Ghana and corresponded with individuals—Ghanaian and non-Ghanaian alike—who had recently visited Ghana or had been affected or exiled by the coup. Writing to Nkrumah in May 1966 from Cairo, Julie Medlock—who up until the coup had served as the director of the Accra-based antinuclear movement, the Accra Assembly—advised the former Ghanaian head of state that she had "just been 'liberated' from Ghana" with her arrival in Cairo and planned to proceed onward to Rome. Medlock then described her experience of the coup. "I spent the day of the coup on a mattress on my bathroom floor," Medlock explained, "listening to the radio orders, soothing my seven kittens, and dodging machine gun bullets." In contrast to most Nkrumah-era projects, the Accra Assembly did not suffer immediate closure following the coup. Instead, the military allowed the antinuclear advocacy program to continue, albeit without funding. However, Medlock advised Nkrumah that she "personally felt that it was ludicrous to try to operate a peace and disarmament Secretariat under a military government, and under these particular circumstances, when you were our Founder."[7] Meanwhile, others sent information about possible deficiencies in the NLC's security systems, purporting to provide openings for an eventual pro-Nkrumah countercoup.[8]

Nkrumah regularly responded to those writing to him with his own interpretations of the events transpiring in Ghana in the aftermath of the coup as well as with accounts of his daily life. In a July 8, 1966, letter to his confidant and literary executor, June Milne, Nkrumah recounted how he had awoken at 4:00 a.m. that morning before transitioning into a discussion of what he portrayed as the deteriorating conditions in Accra under the NLC. Inflation and unemployment, he informed Milne, had resulted in hunger and a series of strikes that he interpreted as "the CPP . . . waking up from its stupefaction."[9] Additionally, throughout his first year in exile, Nkrumah took to Radio Guinea to broadcast into Ghana regular messages to the Ghanaian people. The vast majority of these messages condemned the actions of the NLC, portraying the coup and the resultant military government as pawns of Western imperialism and capitalism. For Nkrumah, the coup was not simply an attack on him, the CPP, and Ghana, but on Africa itself and specifically the pan-African and socialist revolution he envisioned for the continent. "Ghana and the Convention People's Party," he argued in a March 20 broadcast, had "never been forgiven by their enemies for their firm stand and the part they play[ed] in the African revolutionary struggle for emancipation and unity." The result, he continued, was the numerous coup and assassination attempts he endured during his tenure in office. The aim of these neocolonialist and imperialist forces inside and outside the country, as he described them, was to stall and dismantle the political, economic, social, infrastructural, and technical progress his government had brought about inside and outside of Ghana and in turn ensure Africa's continued subjugation.[10]

For Nkrumah, the coup and the imperialist assault on Ghana and Africa he understood the coup as representing were destined to fail. The continent and its peoples, he argued, had been awakened and were ready to fight back.[11] More importantly, Nkrumah's addresses on Radio Guinea marked some of the most prominent indications of key shifts in Nkrumah's political philosophy and particularly in his theory of political action. As historian Ama Biney has described, Nkrumah's exile provided him with an abundance of time to reflect on the state of Africa in the decade following Ghana's 1957 independence.[12] Much had changed in the continent since he had first returned to the Gold Coast in 1947. As discussed in previous chapters, colonialism in the 1940s was a defining, albeit contested, political reality for the vast majority of those living on the continent. Ghana's independence and the broader appeals to African liberation and unity promoted by Nkrumah in the late 1950s had developed out of a diverse group of peoples' faith in the possibilities of African politics in the mid-twentieth century. As a result, by as early as 1960 even the British prime minister, Harold Macmillan, had begun preaching about a "wind of change" sweeping through the continent. Moreover, he even did so to the all-white South African Parliament.[13] By 1966, that wind—as chaotic and unpredictable as it was—had brought independence to nearly the entirety of the continent north of Angola, with almost forty decolonized independent states comprising the continent's contingent in the United Nations. Tied to this wave of independence was a period of political experimentation that featured a number of unique political configurations, alliances, and unions, including those Nkrumah helped forge with countries like Guinea, Mali, and Congo.

By 1966, however, the politics of African decolonization had shifted. In southern Africa, where much of the region still remained under colonial or white minority rule, the prospects of liberation absent armed struggle appeared bleak as white settler states in Rhodesia and South Africa promised to fight any attempt at opening their political systems to Black African majorities. In South Africa specifically, the country's National Party government, which had spent much of the previous decade and a half establishing one of the world's most restrictive systems of racial segregation (apartheid), had mercilessly sought to crack down on the country's Black political movements. By the mid-1960s, key Black South African political figures, including Nelson Mandela, had been jailed and others were in exile. In neighboring Rhodesia (Zimbabwe), the white Rhodesian government responded to international demands that it open pathways to eventual majority rule by unilaterally declaring Rhodesia's independence from Great Britain in November 1965, establishing itself as a pariah state on the international stage. In the nearby Portuguese colonies of Angola and Mozambique, the Portuguese—under the fascist administration of António de Oliveira Salazar—commenced upon a series of brutal wars aimed at destroying the various liberation movements in the colonies. Likewise, in Portuguese West Africa, the Portuguese responded to demands for independence from Guinea-Bissau and Cape Verde by commencing upon a nearly two-decade-long war that would ultimately take the lives of up to two thousand individuals.[14]

In Ghana under Nkrumah, each of these conflicts received regular attention from the Ghanaian government and CPP-run press. As early as 1961, the CPP had already begun accusing the Portuguese of near-genocidal behavior in their colonies, particularly Angola, where, according to the prominent CPP journalist Mabel Dove, "men, women, and children are being shot as game."[15] The *Ghanaian Times* added to Dove's coverage with vivid descriptions of a war of liberation marked by razed villages, starvation, and "babies [dying] in their mothers' arms."[16] Speaking to the United Nations a year later, Alex Quaison-Sackey—the Ghanaian representative to the body—went a step further by accusing the North Atlantic Treaty Organization of propping up the Portuguese in their wars in Angola and elsewhere. As described by Quaison-Sackey, the Angolans' turn to armed struggle in their conflict with the Portuguese was inevitable, for "as a gentle river becomes violent when it is dammed," the Ghanaian diplomat argued, "so does the irresistible flow of nationalism become violent when suppressed."[17]

Linked to the apparently stalled decolonization of southern and Portuguese Africa in Nkrumah's mind was the wave of coups and assassination attempts that began to sweep through the continent in the early 1960s. As noted in chapter 5, the 1961 assassination of Patrice Lumumba disrupted Nkrumah's view of the decolonization process. Two years later, West Africa experienced its first coup with the assassination of Nkrumah's rival in neighboring Togo, Sylvanus Olympio. Questions remain regarding who was responsible for the assassination, with some narratives of the coup tying Nkrumah and the Ghanaian government to the plot.[18] Later that year, the government of Dahomey (Benin) fell in another West African coup. For Nkrumah, who had survived numerous assassination attempts himself, the assassination and coup attempts that appeared to plague the continent in the early and mid-1960s were fundamentally linked to what he perceived to be a rising neocolonial threat to the continent following independence. As he increasingly understood the international dynamics of African independence in the period, former colonial powers, aligned with the United States, viewed independence as an opportunity to experiment with new methods to exploit and disrupt the new nations, allying themselves with, as Nkrumah interpreted them, corrupt and duplicitous officials within the continent. As Nkrumah explained in his 1963 *Africa Must Unite,* neocolonialism "acts covertly, manœuvring [*sic*] men and governments, free of the stigma attached to political rule. It creates client states, independent in name but in point of fact pawns of the very colonial power which is supposed to have given them independence."[19] By early 1966, Nigeria, Algeria, and the Central African Republic would also experience coups.

In the first half of the 1960s, the political instability and rigidity of southern African settler colonialism inserted fissures into Nkrumah's long-held faith in the power of nonviolence as the key to the continent's decolonization strategy. Beginning with the Gold Coast's own path to independence, Nkrumah had long articulated a vision of nonviolence, inspired by the Gandhian movement of the early twentieth century, that foremost aimed to ensure Africa's anticolonial movements the moral high ground in their struggles against colonial rule. Nkrumah argued as early as 1949 that the Gold Coast's anticolonial nationalists, represented by the CPP, had already won the ideological war for decolonization at home and abroad. The challenge that remained was to push back against the remaining "diehard imperialists" in the struggle for complete self-rule without alienating those already sympathetic to the anticolonial cause. To this end, his advocacy of "Positive Action" sought to challenge those supportive of colonial rule by nonviolent, constitutional means, most notably strike actions, boycotts, political agitation, and newspaper campaigns.[20] By the 1958 All-African People's

Conference (AAPC), Nkrumah had broadened and deepened his understanding of the power of nonviolent resistance in the anticolonial cause, presenting it as a central feature of the ontological development of the pan-African revolutionary community cultivated by the decolonization process.[21]

As would happen continuously throughout the era of African decolonization, realities on the ground challenged his ideological, if not philosophical, faith in the principle of nonviolence even as early as the AAPC. At the Accra conference, for instance, Frantz Fanon, speaking on behalf of the Algerian Front de Libération Nationale, would confront Nkrumah on the limits of nonviolence in African decolonization, demanding of his fellow delegates that Africans "should embark on plans effective enough to touch the pulse of the imperialists—by force of action and, indeed, violence."[22] Three years later, Fanon would publish his seminal work, *The Wretched of the Earth,* theorizing the necessity of violence in the decolonization process.[23] For Nkrumah, who as late as 1967 would continue to dismiss Fanon's thought and work as abstract and thus having little in the way of a "practical revolutionary philosophy," an ideal of nonviolent resistance to colonial rule would continue to underpin his philosophy of decolonization throughout his tenure in office.[24] However, even as Nkrumah publicly maintained his faith in nonviolence, he and his administration gradually waded into the politics of armed struggle with the training, arming, and funding of anticolonial Freedom Fighters throughout much of the early 1960s.[25]

The 1966 coup, however, forced Nkrumah into a rethinking of the role of armed struggle in the African liberation movement. For Nkrumah, like Fanon, armed struggle would become a foundational element of the liberation movement in his evolving theory of decolonization. Writing to June Milne in late 1966, Nkrumah advised her of his interest in "raising a volunteer army when I get back to Ghana" and explained that his vision for this army extended beyond Ghana itself. Rather, he viewed it as a pan-African force designed to accelerate the continent's socialist and pan-African transformation. "I have done enough persuasion," he asserted in justifying his objective, "and persuasion must now be backed by a revolutionary armed struggle."[26] Two weeks later, he further explicated the reasoning behind his new faith in armed struggle. For him, a true decolonization had failed on the continent, as neocolonialism ran rampant throughout the continent's newly independent states in the decade since Ghana's independence. "Persuasion and propaganda must be backed by revolutionary armed struggle," he advised her; "the nature and character of neo-colonialism are such that there is no other way to fight and overcome them than by guerilla warfare and struggle."[27] By 1969, Nkrumah was even more definitive in his assessment of the necessity of armed struggle in the African liberation movement as he announced that "there can be no peaceful solution to the problems posed by neo-colonialism. There's only one solution, armed struggle."[28]

* * *

Kwame Nkrumah elaborated on his ideas of armed struggle even more fully in his 1968 *Handbook of Revolutionary Warfare,* his first original full-length book written during his exile.[29] In the *Handbook,* as he regularly referred to it in his writings, Nkrumah foremost sought to retheorize the nature of the global imperialist system and neocolonialism specifically before detailing the structure and strategy of an envisioned armed liberation movement on the continent. Just three years earlier in 1965, Nkrumah had begun to formally unpack and formalize his thoughts on neocolonialism in his *Neo-colonialism: The Last Stage of Imperialism,* a book that would raise the ire of the American government.[30] As with his 1947 *Towards an African Revolution,* Nkrumah turned to V. I. Lenin for inspiration in his dissection of global capitalism. However, *Neo-colonialism* differed from the earlier text in important ways. Both books adopted Lenin's broader emphasis on the capitalist extraction of colonial wealth in their detailing of the inequities and exploitative processes inherent in the colonial system. Yet in *Neo-colonialism,* Nkrumah shifted his focus slightly away from the general processes of capitalist extraction to some of the specific actors, institutions, and corporate bodies he deemed guilty of subverting the continent's already limited political and economic sovereignty. Moreover, in contrast to his previous works, Nkrumah also expanded his imperial field beyond the traditional European colonial powers in *Neo-colonialism*. By 1965, neocolonialism was for Nkrumah a system of exploitation and corruption driven by all capitalist countries, even including those like the United States that historically had proclaimed themselves as anti-imperial.[31]

Much of the rhetoric and analysis found in *Neo-colonialism* had long featured prominently in Ghana's state- and party-run press, particularly in the country's most ideologically minded newspapers like the *Evening News* and the *Spark*. At the international level, the controversy surrounding *Neo-colonialism* in significant part rested in Nkrumah's decision as head of state to eschew diplomatic propriety in the publication of a text that—in contrast to the Ghanaian government's official position—not so indirectly accused those ostensibly allied with Ghana and many other independent African countries of subversion. By the 1968 publication of the *Handbook,* Nkrumah would go even further as he positioned neocolonialism as an intrinsic and fundamental feature of the postwar international system, one that had to be toppled before any form of postliberation reconstruction could begin. He thus opened the book with the declaration that the first step of the liberation process was that all African revolutionaries "KNOW THE ENEMY." He then proceeded to outline what he viewed as the two main objectives of the neocolonial imperialist: "to ensure the continued economic exploitation of our [Africans'] territories" and "to destroy the [African] liberation movement."[32]

As he had previously argued in *Neo-colonialism* and in other texts, in the *Handbook* what chiefly distinguished neocolonialism from its more overt predecessor was the subtlety of its extractive and subversive ambitions. In contrast to the colonialism of the nineteenth and early twentieth centuries, the structure of the postwar global political economy allowed the praxis of neocolonial extraction to be obscured, if not hidden altogether. No longer, Nkrumah argued in the *Handbook*, did what he called the "capitalist-imperialist states"—namely those of Western Europe and the United States—need to rely on control over specific colonies in order to ensure access to both the labor and resources of their subject territories. Rather, these states—working together—transformed imperialism into a collective process in which they used the independence of Africa's recently decolonized states against them, creating client states that were for all intents and purposes dependent on the Western capitalist powers for their political and economic security. What then emerged within Africa's independent states was a political elite more aligned with securing their positions of power than in advancing the interests of the people they governed.[33] Nkrumah would return to this point even more explicitly in 1970 in his final book, *Class Struggle in Africa*. In it, he presented this African ruling and business class—those he termed the "African bourgeoisie"—as "analogous to colonists and settlers." As he argued, they had ultimately embraced the "'hidden hand' of neocolonialism and imperialism" in the support of their own, more localized exploitation of the continent's working and peasant classes.[34]

The response to the new neocolonial threat, Nkrumah insisted, had to be armed struggle. Faced with the newly independent states, the capitalist powers of the West tried to ensure the stability of the political and economic system they sought to build through such means as political, economic, and especially military aid. Military aid took a variety of forms, including technical assistance, "secret" agreements, and special units, among others. Nkrumah asserted that at the heart of all this aid to formerly colonized countries was a process of continued indebtedness and exploitation designed to prop up forces within a given country that were fundamentally "anti-popular." Moreover, as he had done in *Neo-colonialism*, Nkrumah singled out the United States for behavior he deemed fundamentally neocolonial. Following the 1963 assassination of President John F. Kennedy, he argued in the *Handbook*, the United States underwent an important shift in its relations to formerly colonized countries as it invoked, under the leadership of Lyndon Johnson, the rhetoric of "preventative measures" in its pursuit of a policy of "military aggression" against states that operated outside of or against the

United States' Cold War interests.[35] Elsewhere, Nkrumah would suggest that it was this shift in American behavior toward formerly colonized states that led to his ouster, as he accused the United States and Great Britain—in conjunction with the West Germans and Israelis—of being "the initiators of the Ghana coup."[36]

Armed struggle for Nkrumah was thus envisioned as being a freeing action. Much like Fanon's reflection on the necessity of armed struggle in the decolonization process, Nkrumah turned away from the political and nationalist elite in his vision of this struggle and of the African revolution as a whole. Instead, he centered his analysis of the African armed struggle on the revolutionary potential of the peasantry, rural proletariat, and urban working classes. For Fanon, the peasantry represented the natural center of the revolutionary process he imagined for the decolonizing world of the early 1960s.[37] Nkrumah, for his part, would offer a more qualified faith in the inherent revolutionary potential of the peasantry. For him, the peasantry's power largely rested in its numbers. Representing a sleeping giant, the peasantry, Nkrumah insisted, had to be awakened to the material potential and possibilities of the revolution for its force to be felt. He also added that no revolutionary movement had the potential to survive without integrating the peasantry's knowledge and control of the resources of the land. The goal of Nkrumah's envisioned revolutionary movement, then, was to raise the consciousness of the peasantry and bind it to the revolutionary cause through training, education, and investment. Likewise, the rural proletariat—agricultural workers in the continent's various cash crop and other rural industries—promised a revolutionary class familiar with the extractive realities of the colonial capitalist system and one eager to ensure a transformation in their social position and working conditions.[38]

In addition to the peasantry and rural proletariat, Nkrumah also turned to the continent's industrial working classes in the conceptualization of his revolutionary movement. For Fanon, writing nearly a decade earlier, the working classes represented a potential threat to the revolutionary cause due to their proximity to the institutions and values of the colonial system. As a result, he suggested that, much like the colonized middle class and the nationalist parties, the working classes found it difficult to conceptualize a world beyond that created by the colonizer.[39] In many ways, Nkrumah agreed with certain aspects of Fanon's skepticism of the colonized working classes in his own interpretation of their revolutionary potential. For him, the perpetuation of the neocolonial system rested on the continued exploitation and cooperation of the African working class. To this end, he argued, local neocolonial leaders utilized tools like "puppet trade unions" and relatively high wages, among other benefits, in order to ensure the political docility of the African worker. However, Nkrumah also saw Africa's urban working classes as endowed with revolutionary potential that, as with the peasantry, only had to be awakened by guiding the workers toward a greater recognition of their exploitation under the neocolonial system. Moreover, Nkrumah further insisted that the strategic importance of the working classes could not be ignored, for they exhibited a level of mobility—formed through historical processes of rural-to-urban migration—unique on the continent. As a result, Nkrumah presented the urban working classes as a pivotal link connecting the struggles of the African countryside with those of the continent's cities.[40]

Among other segments of African society that Nkrumah looked to in the conceptualization of his revolutionary movement were the continent's students, women, and even "nationalist bourgeoisie," with each group maintaining their own potentialities and challenges in mobilization, education, and training in the goals and methods of the revolution.[41] For Nkrumah, recruitment of revolutionaries from each of Africa's social classes was to come through a range of social and political organizations, including trade unions, peasant organizations, student groups, and women's organizations. Significantly, they were all necessarily to be pan-African in structure and organization, eschewing the political and ideological constraints of the continent's national boundaries. Meanwhile, propaganda and ideological education featured prominently in Nkrumah's envisioned revolutionary army. As he explained in the *Handbook*, propaganda campaigns and ideological education would not only allow the revolutionary movement to distinguish itself from those it deemed as enemies, but would introduce the masses to a theoretical reading of the struggle, rooted in the need for immediate action. In turn, it would awaken the populace to "the need to use force" and marshal the "will to fight."[42]

Training and operations for Nkrumah's revolution were to take place in small guerilla units of ten to twenty-five individuals. Guerillas would study everything from marksmanship and other weaponry skills to bomb making and Morse code. In addition, each fighter in Nkrumah's envisioned army was to be proficient in reading maps and in everyday skills like basic bicycle repair and canoeing, while also having more abstract qualities such as a "strong moral fibre."[43] Nkrumah thus imagined a wave of eager, well-trained, and dedicated clandestine forces capable of disrupting the flow of the African neocolonial system. As he foresaw the revolutionary process, this pan-African revolutionary force would necessarily weaken the hold of governments he and his followers deemed un-African, corrupt, and exploitative, continuously educating and recruiting new and more diverse peoples to the cause and thereby—through their revolutionary actions—building a pan-African and socialist postcolonial Africa from the grassroots.[44]

* * *

In 1968, when Kwame Nkrumah published *The Handbook of Revolutionary Warfare,* his vision of a pan-African revolutionary struggle, let alone of such an army, was aspirational. Despite the security and support of Sékou Touré's government in Guinea, Nkrumah did not have the resources to turn his aspirations into reality. Historians and biographers have therefore cast the ideas presented in the *Handbook* and other texts published during Nkrumah's exile as evidence of an increasing implausibility of his thinking, to the point of self-deception. In his 1988 biography of Nkrumah, David Rooney, for instance, argues that the exiled Nkrumah maintained a wide-ranging "capacity to delude himself" as he promoted, in increasingly abstract terms, the necessity of a socialist pan-African revolution on the continent, while also continuing to believe that those living under military rule in Ghana were simply awaiting his return.[45]

This is a misreading of Nkrumah's time in exile. The *Handbook* and other texts Nkrumah published while in exile represent an attempt at rethinking the envisioned revolution he had undertaken in the Gold Coast nearly two decades earlier. As he indicates throughout his writings during exile, as well as many published during the latter years of his time in Ghana, imperialism proved a much more complicated and nefarious feature of the global order than he had understood as, years earlier, he had sought to bring about the Gold Coast's independence and build a modern, pan-African, and socialist Ghana that would be a model for the continent. Rather than abandon his dream for Ghana and Africa, however,

Nkrumah turned in these writings to questions of praxis and methodology, reexamining the structures of global imperialism and rethinking the types of revolutionary action and commitment needed to dismantle it.

7

Remembering Nkrumah

On April 27, 1972, Kwame Nkrumah died in a Bucharest hospital in the then Socialist Republic of Romania. As early as 1969 in Conakry, as June Milne describes, Nkrumah had been feeling unwell. Doctors diagnosed him with lumbago—lower back pain—and instituted a series of injections to treat it. Nkrumah's condition worsened during the following year, however, and many recommended he seek treatment abroad. Nkrumah refused. By August 1971, when he finally agreed to go, his condition had so deteriorated that he had to be transported to the airport on a stretcher. In Bucharest, doctors said he had been misdiagnosed and thus given the wrong treatment in Conakry. As Milne relates, they "spoke of 'arthrosis'" of the spine. Milne pressed them on whether it was cancer, but the doctors dismissed her question. However, they insisted that, if he had received proper treatment two years earlier, "a simple operation could have cured him."[1]

Nkrumah would spend his last months in the Romanian hospital, regularly communicating with Milne and a few others who were aware of his transport from Conakry. In his first months in Bucharest, Nkrumah would spend much of his time sitting in a chair looking outside at the hospital's garden. According to Milne, during one period he spent six weeks in the chair due to it being too painful to lie down. He lost much of his weight and refused to read, write, watch television, or listen to the radio. As his illness progressed, Nkrumah would spend much of his time on a heavy dose of pain killers. Milne, Sékou Touré, and others devoted much of their energy to putting Nkrumah's affairs in order and trying to arrange for his return to Ghana or at least Africa in his last days. In Ghana, the two-year-old government of the Progress Party—headed by Kofi Busia, a Ghanaian sociologist who had spent much of Nkrumah's tenure in office exiled in Europe—ignored Touré's requests. Following the Busia government's overthrow in early 1972, a delegation sent to Bucharest commissioned by the new military government of I. K. Acheampong concluded that Nkrumah was too ill to travel. Among the delegation was Nkrumah's eldest son, Francis, a doctor at the University of Ghana Medical School. Milne, meanwhile, had been in communication with Julius Nyerere and Kenneth Kaunda in Tanzania and Zambia, respectively, during a trip to East Africa to promote Nkrumah's press, Panaf Books. Both reportedly expressed shock and dismay at the state of Nkrumah's health and interest in inviting him to their countries. No invitations followed. Milne returned to

Bucharest on April 25 to report to Nkrumah on her trip to the continent, only to find him deeply sedated and drifting in and out of consciousness. She received the call notifying her of his death at 8:45 a.m. two days later.[2]

The news of Nkrumah's death spread quickly and widely. The *Times of London,* the *New York Times,* and the *Times of India,* among many other newspapers, ran obituaries of Nkrumah within days of his death.[3] In the United States, where Nkrumah had spent a decade of his life, the *Chicago Defender* and the *Baltimore Afro-American*—two of the country's most prominent Black newspapers—also ran remembrances of Nkrumah in the week following his death. In the *Baltimore Afro-American,* for instance, the prominent local civil rights activist Louise Hines recalled for the newspaper's audience her previous interactions with the former Ghanaian president during his time in the United States. She had first met Nkrumah in 1937 when he traveled to Baltimore to give a lecture at Coppin Normal School (now Coppin State University) on, in her words, "the beauties, the wonders and the crying needs of his native land." To Hines, who would graduate from Coppin that year and would eventually meet Nkrumah again four years later at the University of Pennsylvania, Nkrumah, in his speech, "exhibited that same 'fierce' nationalism which was one of the puzzling aspects of his rule as Ghana's prime minister."[4] Similarly, writing in the *Chicago Defender,* Ethel Payne, one of the leading Black journalists in the country, reflected on Nkrumah's life as a "dream . . . deferred." "Kwame Nkrumah," she told her readers, "was a man of great ambitions. His dreams encompassed the whole of Africa as a powerful, united federation in the family of nations." Returning to the hope of 1957, Payne reproduced in her obituary a portion of the *Defender* article she had written fifteen years earlier describing the excitement of Ghana's independence celebrations, and noted that the dreams and ambitions of 1957 had failed to come to fruition. "If reincarnation is possible," she posited with melancholy, "I have the wistful hope that I can return with the company of those spirits who begat the dream to see its fulfillment. For now, I can indulge in retrospect when pomp and circumstance had their finest hour."[5]

The news of Nkrumah's death reached Ghana in time for the country's newspapers' April 28 editions. However, inside the country, the commemoration of Nkrumah proved tricky for many. Up until his death, Nkrumah had a government-placed bounty on his head. During his exile, this threat had put him in a state of constant danger, leading to the use of pseudonyms for even his deathbed communications.[6] Furthermore, prohibitions had been put in place by post-1966 governments on everything from the Convention People's Party to the display of Nkrumah's image. However, as the *Ghanaian Times* announced Nkrumah's death with a banner headline on April 28, it reported on the National Redemption Council (NRC) government's conciliatory approach to Nkrumah's legacy. Newly established in a January 1972 coup overthrowing Busia's civilian government, the NRC emphasized that Nkrumah's "place in history has been assured as the principal architect of Ghana's independence which hastened the pace of [the] Liberation Movement in Africa." The NRC then continued with the declaration that, "in appreciation of the significant role which Dr. Nkrumah played in the history of this country and in Africa in general," the government was "considering plans to bring his body home for a fitting burial."[7]

For the next several days, coverage of Nkrumah and his death dominated the Ghanaian public sphere as intense debates developed both in public and behind closed doors regarding what to do with his body. In Guinea, Stokely Carmichael (subsequently Kwame Ture)—one of the founders of the Black Power movement in the United States and a regular visitor and student of Nkrumah in Conakry—reported that questions arose as to the competency and the genuineness of the Ghanaian government's professed intentions to properly honor Nkrumah's body and legacy. According to Carmichael's memory of the events, Nkrumah's body had initially been flown to Accra. However, the military government—which Carmichael characterized as "those military CIA stooges"—reportedly refused to allow the plane to land. "Either they were terrified of his corpse or they were paranoid," Carmichael argued, with the Ghanaian government purportedly believing that the "reports of his death were a ruse." It was only once it became clear that Kwame Nkrumah was in fact dead, Carmichael claimed, that the Ghanaians allowed repatriation of Nkrumah's body.[8]

It has been difficult to confirm Carmichael's account of an initial attempted repatriation of Nkrumah's body. However, it does signal a larger distrust among those close to Nkrumah in dealing with the new Ghanaian government. Over the coming days, Sékou Touré would consistently rebuff the Ghanaians' continued proposals to return Nkrumah to Ghana. In doing so, he placed a series of demands on the Ghanaian government to apologize for the 1966 coup overthrowing Nkrumah, but it was unwilling to do so. The Guinean president then responded with plans of his own for a state funeral and burial for Nkrumah in Guinea.[9]

Nkrumah's body was flown to Conakry on April 30. Funeral preparations began swiftly as the Guinean government readied itself for a May 13 and 14 celebration of Nkrumah's life and achievements. In attendance were dignitaries and freedom fighters from throughout the continent and beyond. Amilcar Cabral, who had spent significant time with Nkrumah while both were exiled in Conakry, eulogized Nkrumah. In doing so, Cabral rejected the idea that Nkrumah's death was the result of a bodily malady. "Let no one come and tell us that Nkrumah died from cancer of the throat or any other sickness," Cabral implored his audience. Rather, Nkrumah "was killed by the cancer of betrayal," the betrayal of the revolution that he had sought for Ghana and for Africa. "But we, Africans," Cabral continued, "strongly believe that the dead remain living at our side. We are societies of the living and the dead. Nkrumah," he asserted, "will rise again each dawn in the heart and determination of freedom fighters, in the action of all true African patriots. Nkrumah's immortal spirit presides and will preside at the judgement of history on this decisive phase in our peoples' lives, in life-long struggle against imperialist domination and for the genuine progress of our continent."[10] In his speech, Sékou Touré echoed Cabral. "Kwame Nkrumah was one of the men who mark the destiny of mankind fighting for freedom and dignity," Touré reminded those in attendance. "Kwame Nkrumah lives and will forever because Africa, which is grateful to him, will live forever."[11]

Meanwhile, as Nkrumah's body laid in wake in Conakry, those who had not seen him or who had had little interaction with him since the coup sought to come to terms with his death. Nkrumah's longtime personal secretary, Erica Powell, described the shock she felt at seeing Nkrumah in the coffin. "I felt numb then," she recalled in her memoir of her time working for Nkrumah, "and I still do. It was like being semi-conscious after a major operation, aware in a dreamy sort of way that you have lost something of yourself, but not able to grasp how it will affect you."[12]

The funeral was also the first time his family—Fathia (Rizk) Nkrumah and her three children—had seen Nkrumah since his 1966 overthrow. Living in Cairo since the coup, the family had had limited communications with Nkrumah throughout his exile. As his daughter, Samia Yaba Nkrumah, who was nearly six in February

1966, explained, throughout Nkrumah's exile his children were told that it was not safe for them to visit. "He was a wanted man," she reminded Jacob Gordon, a scholar interviewing her in 2013.[13] For Gamal Nkrumah, the eldest child of Nkrumah's marriage to Fathia, the funeral was an overwhelming experience. As he explained in 1999, the pomp and circumstance of the event was simply too much for a "fourteen-year-old boy to sort out."[14]

As Nkrumah was feted and laid to rest in the National Mausoleum in Conakry, debates raged over his possible return to Ghana. In the eastern Ghanaian border city of Aflao, one woman told the *New York Times* in the days following Nkrumah's death that "we'll go to him only when we know his body is on Ghanaian soil. . . . Nkrumah must come home."[15] In the two weeks leading up to the funeral in Guinea, the Ghanaian press had continued to assert the government's position that Nkrumah would be buried in Ghana and in his hometown of Nkroful specifically. It also claimed that, on his deathbed, "Nkrumah had expressed support for the N.R.C. because," according to the government, "he knew the ousted regime [of Kofi Busia] would do nothing for Ghana."[16] Some also suggested that Nkrumah's burial in Nkroful offered the government an opportunity to transform the small town into a tourist spot.[17] On May 15, the day after the funeral, the *Ghanaian Times* claimed that Nkrumah's body was currently being prepared in Conakry to be flown back to Ghana. At the same time, it reiterated the NRC's calls on Ghanaians in their mourning not to let their emotions get the better of them, to avoid "hurling insults on past political opponents," and to "refrain from questionable activities."[18] A day later, also in the *Ghanaian Times,* the government disputed reports that Nkrumah's body had now been buried in Guinea, claiming that the release of Nkrumah's body to Ghana was still imminent.[19]

After two months of negotiations, Guinea ultimately released Nkrumah's body to Ghana. On July 9, 1972, the Ghanaian government buried Kwame Nkrumah at the site of his birthplace in Nkroful. Two decades later, on July 1, 1992, Nkrumah's body—stolen in the night by the government of Jerry John Rawlings, as some popular accounts in Nkroful explain—was moved again. The government would reinter Nkrumah in Accra

Figure 7.1. Kwame Nkrumah's burial site in Nkroful (1972–92). Photo by author.

in the newly constructed Kwame Nkrumah Mausoleum, built on the site where in 1957 Nkrumah had announced Ghana's independence.

* * *

In the decades since his death, the debates surrounding Kwame Nkrumah and his legacy in Ghana and Africa have not waned. Nearly fifty years after his death, Nkrumah is often still seen in Ghana as having an active role to play in the country's present and future. In March 2019, for instance, columnist Charles Andoh resurrected the popular Convention People's Party slogan that "Nkrumah Never Dies" as he assessed the state of the country on the eve of the sixty-second anniversary of Ghana's independence. Over the past sixty years, the controversial idea that "Nkrumah Never Dies" has taken many meanings, including, in some cases, party-promoted comparisons between Nkrumah and figures like Jesus Christ.[20] However, writing in Ghana's most prominent newspaper, the *Daily Graphic,* Andoh took another approach in his reflections on the phrase. In doing so, he turned readers' attention to Nkrumah's infrastructural and industrial projects. As Andoh explained, many in Ghana reminisce about the Nkrumah era as one of widespread economic, infrastructural, and industrial expansion. "From the north to the south across the east to the west of the country," Andoh recounted, "hundreds of factories ranging from cement, steel, roofing sheets, glass, rubber, jute, matches, sugar, paper and leather to rattan products, were set up under Dr. Nkrumah." However, as Andoh also emphasized, nearly all of these projects are now gone and have been so for a long time.[21]

The power in Andoh's short feature is in its nuance and ambiguity. The idea that "Nkrumah Never Dies" rests in part on the sustainability of Nkrumah's ideas and projects long after he has gone. Andoh subverts the meaning of the phrase, however. As he employs it, the phrase is in part a contemplation of what has been lost. Subsequent governments let the Nkrumah-era projects falter. The harm to the Ghanaian people, Andoh suggests, was real and longstanding. Yet what does remain is the hope, inspiration, and power Nkrumah brought to Ghana and cultivated within the country during the decade and a half he was in power.[22]

Two days later, Kwadwo Afari responded in the *Daily Statesman* with a lament about how "Nkrumah Never Dies." In what could be read as an indirect reply to Andoh, Afari suggested that those who look back with romance to the Nkrumah era were doing so with rose-colored lenses. Much as Kwame Nsiah had argued nearly two decades earlier, on the pronouncement of Nkrumah as Africa's Man of the Millennium, the Nkrumah era for Afari was one of repression, corruption, and fear. It was also one that was fundamentally un-Ghanaian. "Our ancestors lived independent lives outside the control of their chiefs," Afari explained.

Every individual worked for his or her money. They thrived in an environment where consensus building was the norm. In the past and in the present, calls for total victory—in which one side rules continuously and the other group is irrelevant—damage the expectation of true democracy and continued peaceful exchange of power. Nkrumah succeeded in imposing his will on this country, so did Jerry John Rawlings [Ghana's head of state, 1979, 1981–2001] and all those who have tried to capture our individual will and push all of us to adopt a siege/victim mentality.[23]

The arguments that Afari and Nsiah put forward have a long history in twentieth-century Ghana, in some cases dating back to Nkrumah's late-1940s return to the Gold Coast. As already noted, debates surrounding Nkrumah often devolve into dichotomous discussions about whether he was "good" or "bad" for Ghana. Others replicate such a normative assessment in terms of his contribution to Africa. However, Nkrumah and his legacy embody much more than these flattened portrayals of Nkrumah in the Ghanaian, African, and even diasporic political imagination. As Ghanaians and others debate Nkrumah today, the tendency is to adopt Nkrumah and his legacy as a proxy for deeper reflections on the health and structure of the Ghanaian nation or even the pan-African cause. In Nkrumah, they find a figure that personifies the hope and optimism as well as the fear and trepidation of the moment of independence. It was a moment that coupled possibility with uncertainty. It was also a moment in which what it means to be "Ghanaian" and "African" were constantly being redefined, both in relation to and against each other. Sixty-plus years since Ghana's independence, the stakes of these midcentury debates are still shaping the Ghanaian and pan-African scene as Nkrumah and his legacy—both past and present—serve as vehicles through which Ghanaians and others can explore, contest, and reflect on deeper issues of belonging, development, and accumulation in their aspirations for the future. What thus arises through Ghanaians' and others' invocations of Nkrumah is a process of negotiation rooted in the active interaction between the past and the present over the most basic values of the societies they hope to build.

Kwame Nkrumah himself, however, and the complexities and contradictions of the life he lived, often get lost in the broader debates on him and his legacy. Nkrumah's life was a life that transcended boundaries, and that is part of the allure. Part of the first generation of Gold Coasters to come of age under colonial rule, Nkrumah—a child from the small town of Nkroful in Nzemaland in the far southwestern Gold Coast—attended school and, by chance, positioned himself as one of the first students to matriculate into what would become one of the foremost secondary schools in West Africa, Achimota. Several years after graduating from Achimota, Nkrumah took a chance and moved to the United States to attend the first historically Black college in the country, where he survived the final years of the Great Depression and the Second World War as a Black man in a country built upon racial subjugation, segregation, violence, and inequality. Radicalized from his time in the United States, Nkrumah returned to the British imperial sphere in 1945 with the goal of ending colonial rule across Africa and beyond. The fight Nkrumah joined in postwar London ultimately brought him back to the Gold Coast in 1947, where he would spend the next nineteen years imagining, reimagining, and theorizing a world freed from the exploitation and extractive processes of capitalist imperialism. He died in Bucharest twenty-five years later still engaged in that fight.

Notes

Chapter 1: Kwame Nkrumah: A Transnational Life

1 "Kwame Nkrumah's Vision of Africa," BBC World Service, September 14, 2000, https://www.bbc.co.uk /worldservice/people/highlights/000914_nkrumah .shtml. Mandela, for his part, placed fourth in a similar global poll undertaken by the BBC. He finished behind Mahatma Gandhi, Leonardo da Vinci, and Jesus Christ. "Your Millennium: Who Was Your Choice for the Greatest Man of the Last 1000 Years?," BBC News, accessed November 25, 2019, http://news.bbc.co.uk/hi/english /static/events/millennium/default.stm.

2 Kwame Nsiah, "Ghana: The Man of the Millennium," *Ghanaian Chronicle,* January 19, 2000, https://allafrica .com/stories/200001190229.html.

3 Nelson Mandela, quoted in W. Scott Thompson, *Ghana's Foreign Policy, 1957–1966: Diplomacy, Ideology, and the New State* (Princeton, NJ: Princeton University Press, 1969), 222.

4 Stokely Carmichael with Ekwueme Michael Thelwell, *Ready for Revolution: The Life and Struggles of Stokely Carmichael (Kwame Ture)* (New York: Scribner, 2003), 81, 115.

5 See Jeffrey S. Ahlman, *Living with Nkrumahism: Nation, State, and Pan-Africanism in Ghana* (Athens: Ohio University Press, 2017).

6 On Sankara, see Ernest Harsch, *Thomas Sankara: An African Revolutionary* (Athens: Ohio University Press, 2014).

7 Staffan I. Lindberg, *Democracy and Elections in Africa* (Baltimore: Johns Hopkins University Press, 2006), 14.

8 Ahlman, *Living with Nkrumahism,* esp. 206–11.

9 Ali Mazrui, "Nkrumah: The Leninist Czar," *Transition,* no. 26 (1966): 17.

10 Kwame Nkrumah, *Ghana: The Autobiography of Kwame Nkrumah* (Edinburgh: Thomas Nelson and Sons, 1957). See also Philip Holden, *Autobiography and Decolonization: Modernity, Masculinity, and the Nation-State* (Madison: University of Wisconsin Press, 2008), 117–41.

11 Ahlman, *Living with Nkrumahism,* 16–22.

Chapter 2: Empire and a Colonial Youth

1 For more in-depth discussions of the years leading to Ghana's independence, see Dennis Austin, *Politics in Ghana, 1946–1960* (London: Oxford University Press, 1964); Jean Marie Allman, *The Quills of the Porcupine: Asante Nationalism in an Emergent Ghana* (Madison: University of Wisconsin Press, 1993); Richard Rathbone, *Nkrumah and the Chiefs: The Politics of Chieftaincy in Ghana, 1951–1960* (Athens: Ohio University Press, 2000); and Jeffrey S. Ahlman, *Living with Nkrumahism: Nation, State, and Pan-Africanism in Ghana* (Athens: Ohio University Press, 2017), esp. 49–83.

2 Kwame Nkrumah, speech at the independence of Ghana, March 6, 1957, excerpted in Kwame Nkrumah, *I Speak of Freedom: A Statement of African Ideology* (New York: Frederick A. Praeger, 1961), 107.

3 Kwame Nkrumah, *Africa Must Unite* (London: Heinemann, 1963), 32.

4 I explore many of the themes outlined in the following four paragraphs in more depth in another current book project, *Ghana: A Modern History,* to be published by I. B. Tauris.

5 Jean Barbot, *Barbot on Guinea: The Writings of Jean Barbot on West Africa, 1678–1712,* ed. P. E. H. Hair, Adam Jones, and Robin Law (London: Hakluyt Society, 1992), 2:333.

6 "Embarkation Regions, 1600–1699, Yearly," *Voyages: The Trans-Atlantic Slave Trade Database*, accessed October 17, 2018, http://www.slavevoyages.org/estimates /yWOdwBog.

7 "Embarkation Regions, 1700–1799, Yearly," *Voyages: The Trans-Atlantic Slave Trade Database*, accessed October 17, 2018, http://www.slavevoyages.org/estimates /yWOdwBog.

8 Kwame Nkrumah, *Ghana: The Autobiography of Kwame Nkrumah* (Edinburgh: Thomas Nelson and Sons, 1957), 3–10, quote on 7.

9 Nkrumah, *Ghana,* 11.

10 C. K. Graham, *The History of Education in Ghana: From the Earliest Times to the Declaration of Independence* (London: Frank Cass, 1971), 1–5.

11 Government of the Gold Coast, *Blue Book, 1850* (London: Her Majesty's Stationery Office, 1850), 84–85, 94; Government of the Gold Coast, *Blue Book, 1899* (London: Her Majesty's Stationery Office, 1899), V1–V9; Graham, *History of Education in Ghana,* 51–56.

12 Colony of the Gold Coast, *Report on the Census for the Year 1901* (London: Waterlow and Sons, 1902), 4.

13 Jean Allman and Victoria Tashjian, *"I Will Not Eat Stone": A Women's History of Colonial Asante* (Portsmouth, NH: Heinemann, 2000), esp. 90–91.

14 Nkrumah, *Ghana,* 11–12.

15 "The Larger Life Education," *Gold Coast Leader,* May 11, 1907.

16 Thomas Fowell Buxton, *The African Slave Trade and Its Remedy* (London: John Murray, 1840), 454.

17 On how these values were expressed in some of the Gold Coast's schools in the late nineteenth and early twentieth centuries, see, for instance, Stephan F. Miescher, *Making Men in Ghana* (Bloomington: Indiana University Press, 2005), 56–76.

18 Nkrumah, *Ghana,* 12–13.

19 Miescher, *Making Men in Ghana,* 61–63; Stephan F. Miescher, "The Life Histories of Boakye Yiadom (Akasease

Kofi of Abetifi, Kwawu): Exploring the Subjectivity and 'Voices' of a Teacher-Catechist in Colonial Ghana," in *African Words, African Voices: Critical Practices in Oral History,* ed. Luise White, Stephan F. Miescher, and David William Cohen (Bloomington: Indiana University Press, 2001), 170.

20 Nkrumah, *Ghana,* 12–13.

21 Frederick Gordon Guggisberg, quoted in H. O. A. McWilliam and M. A. Kwamena-Poh, *The Development of Education in Ghana: An Outline,* new ed. (London: Longman, 1975), 54; also quoted in Cati Coe, "Educating an African Leadership: Achimota and the Teaching of African Culture in the Gold Coast," *Africa Today* 49, no. 3 (2002): 27–28.

22 William Malcolm Hailey, *An African Survey: A Study of Problems Arising in Africa South of the Sahara* (London: Oxford University Press, 1938), 1207, 1249.

23 Frederick Gordon Guggisberg, quoted in R. E. Wraith, *Guggisberg* (London: Oxford University Press, 1967), 100.

24 David Kimble, *A Political History of Ghana: The Rise of Gold Coast Nationalism, 1850–1928* (Oxford: Clarendon, 1963), 441–42.

25 Frederick Gordon Guggisberg, Legislative Council Debates, February 22, 1926, in G. E. Metcalfe, ed., *Great Britain and Ghana: Documents of Ghana History, 1807–1957* (London: Thomas Nelson and Sons, 1964), 600.

26 J. E. K. Aggrey, "The Prince of Wales College: A 'Wireless' Talk from London," *Southern Workman* 55, no. 1 (January 1926): 40–41. Aggrey's wife, Rose Douglas Aggrey, read large portions of Aggrey's paper to the wireless audience, including the quoted sections.

27 Nkrumah, *Ghana,* 19–20.

28 Coe, "Educating an African Leadership," 24.

29 Nkrumah, *Ghana,* 18, 20–21.

30 Nkrumah, 20–21.

31 Nkrumah, 13.

32 Nkrumah, 21.

33 Nkrumah, 17–18.

Chapter 3: Diasporic Connections and Anticolonial Experimentation

1 Kwame Nkrumah, *Ghana: The Autobiography of Kwame Nkrumah* (Edinburgh: Thomas Nelson and Sons, 1957), 22–23.

2 J. C. Zizer, *West African Nationhood*, July 10, 1931, and December 10, 1930, quoted in J. Ayodele Langley, *Pan-Africanism and Nationalism in West Africa, 1900–1945: A Study in Ideology and Social Classes* (Oxford: Clarendon, 1973), 183.

3 Bankole Timothy, *Kwame Nkrumah: His Rise to Power* (London: George Allen & Unwin, 1955), 22–23; Marika Sherwood, *Kwame Nkrumah: The Years Abroad, 1935–1947* (Legon, Ghana: Freedom Publications, 1996), 21.

4 Nkrumah, *Ghana*, 23–27.

5 Nkrumah, 29.

6 See Robin D. G. Kelley, *Race Rebels: Culture, Politics, and the Black Working Class* (New York: Free Press, 1996), 123–58.

7 C. L. R. James, *A History of Pan-African Revolt* (Chicago: Charles H. Kerr, 1995), 108–10; originally published as *A History of Negro Revolt* (1938).

8 See S. K. B. Asante, *Pan-African Protest: West Africa and the Italo-Ethiopian Crisis, 1934–1941* (London: Longman, 1977), esp. 98–171; William R. Scott, *The Sons of Sheba's Race: African-Americans and the Italo-Ethiopian War, 1935–1941* (Bloomington: Indiana University Press, 1993); Brent Hayes Edwards, *The Practice of Diaspora: Literature, Translation, and the Rise of Black Internationalism* (Cambridge: Harvard University Press, 2003), 296–300; and Hakim Adi, *Pan-Africanism and Communism: The Communist International, Africa and the Diaspora, 1919–1939* (Trenton, NJ: Africa World Press, 2013), 174–86.

9 Leslie James, *George Padmore and Decolonization from Below: Pan-Africanism, the Cold War, and the End of Empire* (New York: Palgrave Macmillan, 2015), 30. The IAFE is also often referred to as the International African Friends of Abyssinia.

10 *Gold Coast Spectator,* quoted in Adi, *Pan-Africanism and Communism,* 176.

11 Horace Mann Bond, *Education for Freedom: A History of Lincoln University, Pennsylvania* (Lincoln University, PA: Lincoln University, 1976), 488–97; Sherwood, *Kwame Nkrumah,* 29.

12 Bond, *Education for Freedom,* 501.

13 Sherwood, *Kwame Nkrumah,* 21.

14 Nkrumah, *Ghana,* 32.

15 For Azikiwe's perspectives on his membership in Phi Beta Sigma, see Nnamdi Azikiwe, *My Odyssey: An Autobiography* (London: C. Hurst, 1970), 133–35.

16 Nkrumah, *Ghana,* 32.

17 Polly Hill, *The Gold Coast Cocoa Farmer: A Preliminary Survey* (London: Oxford University Press, 1956), 133.

18 "Farmers and Cocoa (1)," *African Morning Post,* October 1, 1937.

19 Gwendolyn Mikell, *Cocoa and Chaos in Ghana* (Washington, DC: Howard University Press, 1992), 144.

20 Gareth Austin, *Labour, Land, and Capital in Ghana: From Slavery to Free Labour in Asante, 1807–1956* (Rochester, NY: University of Rochester Press, 2005), 245.

21 E. Y. (Yip) Harburg, quoted in Studs Terkel, *Hard Times: An Illustrated Oral History of the Great Depression* (New York: New Press, 1986), 23.

22 Thomas H. Coode and John F. Bauman, *People, Poverty, and Politics: Pennsylvanians during the Great Depression* (Lewisburg, PA: Bucknell University Press, 1981), 55, 181.

23 University of Massachusetts Amherst Libraries, Special Collections and University Archives, W. E. B. Du Bois Papers (MS 312), W. E. Burghardt Du Bois, "Progress by Poverty," Chicago, February 12, 1939.

24 W. E. B. Du Bois, *The Philadelphia Negro: A Social Study* (Philadelphia: Publications of the University of Pennsylvania, 1899), 47.

25 Charles Pete T. Banner-Haley, *To Do Good and To Do Well: Middle-Class Blacks and the Depression, Philadelphia, 1929–1941* (New York: Garland, 1993), 45.

26 Banner-Haley, *To Do Good and To Do Well,* 51; Coode and Bauman, *People, Poverty, and Politics,* 55.

27 Mark Naison, *Communists in Harlem during the Depression* (Urbana: University of Illinois Press, 1983), 31.

28 Nkrumah, *Ghana,* 38.

29 Nkrumah, 36–39, quote on 37.

30 Adam Ewing, *The Age of Garvey: How a Jamaican Activist Created a Mass Movement and Changed Global Black Politics* (Princeton, NJ: Princeton University Press, 2014), 148–49.

31 "Report of UNIA Meeting," April 29, 1920, in *The Marcus Garvey and Universal Negro Improvement Association Papers,* ed. Robert A. Hill, vol. 2, *27 August 1919–31 August 1920* (Berkeley: University of California Press, 1983), 299; E. David Cronon, *Black Moses: The Story of Marcus Garvey and the Universal Negro Improvement Association,* 2nd ed. (Madison: University of Wisconsin Press, 1969), 67–69; Colin Grant, *Negro with a Hat: The Rise and Fall of Marcus Garvey* (Oxford: Oxford University Press, 2008), 201–2.

32 Lionel Francis, quoted in Cronon, *Black Moses,* 165.

33 Kobina Sekyi, "The Parting of Ways," unpublished ms. ca. 1915, in *The Marcus Garvey and Universal Negro Improvement Association Papers,* ed. Robert A. Hill, vol. 10, *Africa for the Africans, 1923–1945* (Berkeley: University of California Press, 2006), 353–55, quote on 354.

34 Marcus Garvey, *The Philosophy and Opinions of Marcus Garvey,* 2 vols., ed. Amy Jacques-Garvey (New York: Universal Publishing, 1923–25); Grant, *Negro with a Hat,* 354.

35 Nkrumah, *Ghana,* 45–46.

36 V. I. Lenin, *Imperialism: The Highest Stage of Capitalism: A Popular Outline,* rev. trans. (Moscow: Co-operative Publishing Society of Foreign Workers in the USSR, 1934); Kwame Nkrumah, *Towards Colonial Freedom: Africa in the Struggle against World Imperialism* (London: Farleigh, 1947); Kwame Nkrumah, *Neo-colonialism: The Last Stage of Imperialism* (London: Thomas Nelson, 1965).

37 Nkrumah, *Ghana,* 45.

38 Gretchen Gerzina, *Black London: Life before Emancipation* (New Brunswick, NJ: Rutgers University Press, 1995), 3.

39 Jonathan Schneer, *London 1900: The Imperial Metropolis* (New Haven, CT: Yale University Press, 1999), 3–14, 203–26; Hakim Adi, *West Africans in Britain 1900–1960: Nationalism, Pan-Africanism and Communism* (London: Lawrence & Wishart, 1998), 9–13.

40 Joseph Appiah, *Joe Appiah: The Autobiography of an African Patriot* (Accra: Asempa, 1990), 145–89. For a broader discussion of WASU, see Adi, *West Africans in Britain.*

41 Nkrumah, *Ghana,* 50–51.

42 For a broader discussion of Padmore's role in Nkrumah's government and the office that emerged out of his work, see Jeffrey S. Ahlman, "Managing the Pan-African Workplace: Discipline, Ideology, and the Cultural Politics of the Ghanaian Bureau of African Affairs, 1959–1966," *Ghana Studies,* nos. 15/16 (2012–13): 337–71; James, *George Padmore and Decolonization from Below,* 164–90; and Matteo Grilli, *Nkrumaism and African Nationalism: Ghana's Pan-African Foreign Policy in the Age of Decolonization* (New York: Palgrave Macmillan, 2018), 33–122.

43 James, *George Padmore and Decolonization from Below,* 22–34, 78–82.

44 Nkrumah, *Ghana,* 49–50.

45 George Padmore, "Scramble over African Colonies Takes Place between Representatives of Big 5," *West African Pilot,* October 20, 1945.

46 George Padmore, "European Imperialists Ponder! Let Us Drain Africa before It Is Too Late, They Say," *Ashanti Pioneer,* July 16, 1947.

47 Franklin D. Roosevelt and Winston Churchill, "The Atlantic Charter," August 14, 1941, reproduced in Douglas Brinkley and David R. Facey-Crowther, *The Atlantic Charter* (New York: St. Martin's Press, 1994), xvii–xviii.

48 Bonny Ibhawoh, "Second World War Propaganda, Imperial Idealism, and Anti-colonial Nationalism in British West Africa," *Nordic Journal of African Studies* 16, no. 2 (2007): 240–41.

49 Nnamdi Azikiwe, address delivered at the plenary session of the British Peace Congress held at the Lime Grove Baths, Goldhawk Road, Hammersmith, London, on October 23, 1949, reproduced in Nnamdi Azikiwe, *Zik: A Selection from the Speeches of Nnamdi Azikiwe* (Cambridge: Cambridge University Press, 1961), 61–62, quote on 62. For a fuller discussion of the ways in which the question of self-determination framed twentieth-century African political debates, see Adom Getachew, *Worldmaking after Empire: The Rise and Fall of Self-Determination* (Princeton, NJ: Princeton University Press, 2019).

50 "Declaration of the Colonial Workers, Farmers, and Intellectuals," in George Padmore, ed., *Colonial and Coloured Unity: A Programme of Action: History of the Pan-African Congress* (London: Hammersmith Bookshop, 1963), 6; first edition published 1947 by the Pan-African Federation, Manchester, United Kingdom.

51 "The Challenge to the Colonial Powers," in Padmore, *Colonial and Coloured Unity,* 5.

52 Nkrumah, *Ghana,* 54; Kwame Nkrumah, *Revolutionary Path* (London: Panaf, 1973), 42–43. One of Nkrumah's biographers, Marika Sherwood, questions Nkrumah's claim of authorship, arguing that the Manchester Congress's declarations were likely collaborative efforts; Sherwood, *Kwame Nkrumah,* 122.

53 Kwame Nkrumah, "Imperialism in North and West Africa," October 16, 1945, in Padmore, *Colonial and Coloured Unity,* 32.

54 Nkrumah, *Towards Colonial Freedom,* 6–8, quote on 6.

55 [T.] Ras Makonnen, *Pan-Africanism from Within,* rec. and ed. Kenneth King (London: Oxford University Press, 1973), 178–94.

56 Bankole Awooner-Renner, *West African Soviet Union* (London: WANS Press, 1946).

Chapter 4: Between Nation and Pan-Africanism: Part I

1 Kwame Nkrumah, *Ghana: The Autobiography of Kwame Nkrumah* (Edinburgh: Thomas Nelson and Sons, 1957), 60–61.

2 Colonial Office, *Report of the Commission of Enquiry into Disturbances in the Gold Coast, 1948* (London: His Majesty's Stationery Office, 1948), 17–18.

3 Dennis Austin, *Politics in Ghana, 1946–1960* (London: Oxford University Press, 1964), 52–53.

4 Richard Rathbone, introduction to Richard Rathbone, ed., *Ghana*, vol. 1, pt. 1, of *British Documents on the End of Empire*, ser. B (London: Her Majesty's Stationery Office, 1992), xxxv, lxx.

5 K. G. Bradley to [Arthur] Creech Jones, minutes by J. K. Thompson and Sir T. Lloyd, December 12, 1947, in Rathbone, *Ghana*, 42, 45.

6 Nkrumah, *Ghana*, 62.

7 For a more in-depth discussion of the context and events surrounding Nkrumah's return to the Gold Coast, see Jeffrey S. Ahlman, *Living with Nkrumahism: Nation, State, and Pan-Africanism in Ghana* (Athens: Ohio University Press, 2017), 6–10, 49–54.

8 Colonial Office, *Report of the Commission*, 38–39.

9 Keri Grace Lambert, "Elastic Allegiances: Rubber, Development, and the Production of Sovereignties in Ghana, 1880–2017" (PhD diss., Yale University, 2019), 119–53, 151–52; Keri Lambert, "'In the Nature of a Crusade': Wartime Extraction and the Seeds of Industrialization in the Gold Coast," *Journal of West African History* 6, no. 1 (2020): 63–90.

10 David Killingray, "Military and Labour Recruitment in the Gold Coast during the Second World War," *Journal of African History* 23, no. 1 (1982): 83–95.

11 David Killingray, "Soldiers, Ex-servicemen, and Politics in the Gold Coast, 1939–50," *Journal of Modern African Studies* 21, no. 3 (1983): 529–32.

12 Colonial Office, *Report of the Commission*, 10–15.

13 Joseph Boakye Danquah, "The Moment of Decision: A Speech Delivered at the Inaugural Meeting of the United Gold Coast Convention, at Saltpond, on 4 August 1947," in Joseph Boakye Danquah, *Historic Speeches and Writings on Ghana*, comp. H. K. Akyeampong (Accra: George Boakie, 1970), 48.

14 Dennis Austin, "The Working Committee of the United Gold Coast Convention," *Journal of African History* 2, no. 2 (1961): 284.

15 Colonial Office, *Report of the Commission,* 18.

16 "Agitation," *Evening News,* September 3, 1948.

17 Rathbone, introduction to Rathbone, *Ghana,* xlix; Ahlman, *Living with Nkrumahism,* 54–55.

18 Resolutions of the Working Committee of the UGCC, June 11, 1949, quoted in Dennis Austin, "Working Committee," 291.

19 Mensa Abrompa, "The People's Declaration," *Evening News,* July 22, 1949.

20 "You," *Evening News,* July 22, 1949.

21 Kwame Nkrumah, *What I Mean by Positive Action* (Accra: Convention People's Party, [1949]), 4.

22 Dennis Austin, *Politics in Ghana,* 89–91, 103, 141.

23 Yale University Library, Archives and Manuscripts, Group No. 1519, box 1, folder 10, United Gold Coast Convention, *Ten-Point Programme and Re-Affirmation of Policy: National Consultative Conference, Cape Coast, May 13, 1950* (Saltpond: United Gold Coast Convention, 1950), 4; Ghana Congress Party, *Manifesto of the Ghana Congress Party* ([1950]), 3.

24 Yale University Beinecke Rare Book and Manuscript Library, Richard Wright Papers, box 22, folder 344, Richard Wright Travel Journal, July 26, 1953.

25 Public Records and Archives Administration Department [hereafter cited as PRAAD]-Accra, Administrative Files 16/23, "Speech Delivered by Osagyefo Kwame Nkrumah, President of Ghana, at the Opening of the Hall of Trade Unions, 9 July 1960."

26 Ama Biney, *The Political and Social Thought of Kwame Nkrumah* (New York: Palgrave Macmillan, 2011), 59–60.

27 Statement of Kumasi Congress, quoted in "Congress at Kumasi: Nationalists Meet in the Gold Coast to Lay Plans for West African Co-operation," *West African Review,* February 1954.

28 "Congress of Kumasi," *West African Review,* February 1954.

29 Dennis Austin, *Politics in Ghana*, 200–201; Biney, *Political and Social Thought*, 60–61.

30 "Pan-Africa: International Confab Here," *Evening News*, April 18, 1957. On South Africa's refusal to participate, see W. Scott Thompson, *Ghana's Foreign Policy, 1957–1966: Diplomacy, Ideology, and the New State* (Princeton, NJ: Princeton University Press, 1969), 32.

31 Thompson, *Ghana's Foreign Policy*, 31–34.

32 PRAAD-Accra, Record Group [hereafter cited as RG] 8/2/772, "Speech by the Prime Minister to the Conference of Independent African States, 15th April, 1958," in *Conference of Independent African States: Confidential Report/Conférence d'États Africains Indépendants: Rapport Confidentiel*, 1–13, quote on 8.

33 PRAAD-Accra RG 8/2/772, "Speech by Dr. Kwame Nkrumah, Prime Minister of Ghana and Chairman of the Conference of Independent African States at the Final Session of the Conference on Tuesday, 22nd April, 1958," in *Conference of Independent African States: Confidential Report/Conférence d'États Africains Indépendants: Rapport Confidentiel*, 95–96 (emphasis in original).

34 "Speech by the Prime Minister of Ghana at the Opening Session of the All-African People's Conference on Monday, 8th December 1958," in All-African People's Conference, *Speeches by the Prime Minister of Ghana at the Opening and Closing Sessions on December 8th and 13th, 1958* (Accra: Community Centre, 1958), 1.

35 Thompson, *Ghana's Foreign Policy*, 68. On Guinea's independence, see Elizabeth Schmidt, *Mobilizing the Masses: Gender, Ethnicity, and Class in the Nationalist Movement in Guinea, 1939–1958* (Portsmouth, NH: Heinemann, 2005), 171–96; Elizabeth Schmidt, *Cold War and Decolonization in Guinea, 1946–1958* (Athens: Ohio University Press, 2007), 125–86.

36 Thompson, *Ghana's Foreign Policy*, 67–73, 150–52; Matteo Grilli, *Nkrumaism and African Nationalism: Ghana's Pan-African Foreign Policy in the Age of Decolonization* (New York: Palgrave Macmillan, 2018), 85–94, 216–19, 247;

Kwame Nkrumah, *The Challenge of the Congo* (London: Thomas Nelson and Sons, 1967), 30–31.

37 Jeffrey S. Ahlman, "Managing the Pan-African Workplace: Discipline, Ideology, and the Cultural Politics of the Ghanaian Bureau of African Affairs, 1959–1966," *Ghana Studies,* nos. 15/16 (2012–13): 337–71; Grilli, *Nkrumaism and African Nationalism.*

38 Maya Angelou, *All God's Children Need Traveling Shoes* (New York: Vintage Books, 1991), 39.

39 George Padmore Research Library on African Affairs [hereafter cited as GPRL], Bureau of African Affairs [hereafter cited as BAA]/Research Library on African Affairs [hereafter cited as RLAA]/811, Adelino Chitofo Guambe to Kwame Nkrumah, Bulawayo, Southern Rhodesia, December 13, 1960.

40 GPRL, BAA/RLAA/633, Ntsu Mokhehle to Kwame Nkrumah, Maseru, Basutoland, April 30, 1959.

41 GPRL, BAA/RLAA/348, E. T. Makiwane to Secretary of the A.A.T.U.F., Wami, Nigeria, June 4, 1960.

42 Nkrumah, speech at the independence of Ghana, March 6, 1957, excerpted in Kwame Nkrumah, *I Speak of Freedom: A Statement of African Ideology* (New York: Frederick A. Praeger, 1961), 107.

43 Kwame Nkrumah, June 21, 1963, in Government of Ghana, National Assembly, *Parliamentary Debates,* vol. 32 (Accra: State Publishing Company, 1963), col. 85.

Chapter 5: Between Nation and Pan-Africanism: Part II

1 Rosalyn Higgins, *United Nations Peacekeeping, 1946–1967: Documents and Commentary,* vol. 3, *Africa* (Oxford: Oxford University Press, 1980), 88.

2 Jeffrey S. Ahlman, "The Algerian Question in Nkrumah's Ghana, 1958–1960: Debating 'Violence' and 'Nonviolence' in African Decolonization," *Africa Today* 57, no. 2 (2010): 78–81.

3 Philip E. Muehlenbeck, *Betting on the Africans: John F. Kennedy's Courting of African Nationalist Leaders*

(Oxford: Oxford University Press, 2012), 143–44; Jeffrey S. Ahlman, *Living with Nkrumahism: Nation, State, and Pan-Africanism in Ghana* (Athens: Ohio University Press, 2017), 177.

4 George Padmore Research Library on African Affairs, Bureau of African Affairs/Research Library on African Affairs/370, Kwame Nkrumah to Bakary Djibo, Accra, June 29, 1960.

5 Ahlman, *Living with Nkrumahism,* 14, 141–42.

6 Kwame [Francis Nwia-Kofi] Nkrumah, "Education and Nationalism in Africa," *Educational Outlook* 18, no. 1 (1943): 38.

7 See, for instance, "Educate Our Women," *Evening News,* September 3, 1948; "Gov't and Female Education," *Evening News,* December 4, 1948; and "Barton and Mass Education," *Evening News,* January 28, 1949.

8 See the speech given in the National Assembly on June 13, 1957, by Minister of Education C. T. Nylander, in Government of Ghana, National Assembly, *Parliamentary Debates,* vol. 6, cols. 820–23; Betty Stein George, *Education in Ghana* (Washington, DC: Government Printing Office, 1976), 43; and Ahlman, *Living with Nkrumahism,* 55, 235n23.

9 Abena Dove Osseo-Asare, "Scientific Equity: Experiments in Laboratory Education in Ghana," *Isis: Journal of the History of Science Society* 104, no. 4 (2013): 739. See also Jonathan Zimmerman, "'Money, Materials, and Manpower': Ghanaian In-Service Teacher Education and the Political Economy of Failure, 1961–1971," *History of Education Quarterly* 51, no. 1 (2011): 1–27.

10 Jeffrey S. Ahlman, "Africa's Kitchen Debate: Ghanaian Domestic Space in the Age of Cold War," in *Gender, Sexuality, and the Cold War: A Global Perspective,* ed. Philip E. Muehlenbeck (Nashville, TN: Vanderbilt University Press, 2017), 166–69.

11 Bankole Timothy, "New Deal in Education: A Critique," *Daily Graphic,* November 15, 1952.

12 S. G. Antor, in Government of Ghana, National Assembly, *Parliamentary Debates,* June 13, 1957, vol. 6, col. 833.

13 W. Ntoso, in Government of Ghana, National Assembly, *Parliamentary Debates,* June 13, 1957, vol. 6, col. 843.

14 Jatoe Kaleo, in Government of Ghana, National Assembly, *Parliamentary Debates,* August 13, 1958, vol. 11, col. 1447.

15 Kwame Arhin, *A View of Kwame Nkrumah, 1909–1972: An Interpretation* (Accra: Sedco, 1990), dedication (emphasis in original).

16 George, *Education in Ghana,* 51.

17 Public Records and Archives Administration Department (hereafter cited as PRAAD)-Accra, Administrative Files (hereafter cited as ADM) 13/2/4, Minister of Housing and Town and Country Planning, "Acquisition of the Land for Tema Township," February 28, 1952; Keith Jopp, *Tema: Ghana's New Town and Harbour* (Accra: Ministry of Information and Broadcasting, 1961), 8.

18 On Nkrumah's plans for Tema and the popular reactions to it, see Ahlman, *Living with Nkrumahism,* 60–73.

19 Stephan F. Miescher, "'Nkrumah's Baby': The Akosombo Dam and the Dream of Development in Ghana, 1952–1966," *Water History* 6, no. 4 (2014): 343, 344.

20 Sir Robert Jackson, "The Volta River Project," *Progress: Unilever Quarterly* 50, no. 282 (1964): 2.

21 Stephan F. Miescher, "'No One Should Be Worse Off': The Akosombo Dam, Modernization, and the Experience of Resettlement in Ghana," in *Modernization as Spectacle in Africa,* ed. Peter J. Bloom, Takyiwaa Manuh, and Stephan F. Miescher (Bloomington: Indiana University Press, 2014), 187–91.

22 "No, You Can't Have Your Industries: How Nkrumah's Dream to Industrialise Ghana as a Model for the Whole of Africa Was Frustrated," *New African,* no. 404 (February 2002): 19.

23 Miescher, "'Nkrumah's Baby,'" 349–55.

24 Kwame Kwarteng, quoted in Osei Boateng, "Nkrumah Surely Must Be Turning in His Grave," *New African,* no. 404 (2002): 20. Boateng's article is largely a reprinted transcription of the fifth part of the 1992 BBC

documentary titled *Pandora's Box: A Fable from the Age of Science,* episode title "Black Power."

25 Yale University Beinecke Rare Book and Manuscript Library, Richard Wright Papers, box 5, folder 81, Richard Wright, "The Birth of a Man and the Birth of a Nation," unpublished MS, [1957?]; Richard Wright, *Black Power: A Record of Reactions in a Land of Pathos* (New York: Harper and Brothers, 1954).

26 Miescher, "'No One Should Be Worse Off,'" 191–98; Ahlman, *Living with Nkrumahism,* 60–73.

27 Keri Lambert, "'It's All Work and Happiness on the Farms': Agricultural Development between the Blocs in Nkrumah's Ghana," *Journal of African History* 60, no. 1 (2019): 37–42.

28 Ahlman, *Living with Nkrumahism,* 131–32.

29 J. B. Danquah, in Government of the Gold Coast, Legislative Assembly, *Legislative Assembly Debates,* March 9, 1954, issue no. 1, col. 1461.

30 Miescher, "'Nkrumah's Baby,'" 355–58.

31 Abayifaa Karbo, in Government of Ghana, National Assembly, *Parliamentary Debates,* February 22, 1961, vol. 22, cols. 157–60.

32 K. A. Gbedemah, in Government of Ghana, National Assembly, *Parliamentary Debates,* February 22, 1961, vol. 22, col. 159.

33 Grace Ayensu, in Government of Ghana, National Assembly, *Parliamentary Debates,* February 22, 1961, vol. 22, col. 161.

34 John Arjarquah, in Government of Ghana, National Assembly, *Parliamentary Debates,* February 22, 1961, vol. 22, col. 162.

35 Yaw Asare, "Ghana Educational Programme," *Evening News,* July 26, 1949; F. V. A. Appiah, "I Am Fed Up with the African Imperialists," *Evening News,* October 6, 1949.

36 "Nkrumah Deserves the Name Messiah—Ako Adjei," *Evening News,* January 9, 1962.

37 Arhin, *Kwame Nkrumah,* 31.

38 Moses T. Agyeman-Anane, "National Charges against Mr. Kwame Nkrumah," quoted in Jean Marie Allman, *The Quills of the Porcupine: Asante Nationalism in an Emergent Ghana* (Madison: University of Wisconsin Press, 1993), 36.

39 PRAAD-Accra, Record Group 17/2/689, unknown to Nkrumah, Anloga, March 23, 1956; Ahlman, *Living with Nkrumahism*, 77–78.

40 Jeffrey S. Ahlman, "A New Type of Citizen: Youth, Gender, and Generation in the Ghanaian Builders Brigade," *Journal of African History* 53, no. 1 (2012): 99 and, more broadly, 98–102.

41 R. R. Amponsah, in Government of Ghana, National Assembly, *Parliamentary Debates,* July 14, 1958, col. 423. On the Preventative Detention Act more broadly, Ahlman, *Living with Nkrumahism,* 179–81.

42 For a discussion of the case of Amponsah, Apaloo, and Awhaitey, see Jeffrey S. Ahlman, "'The Strange Case of Major Awhaitey': Conspiracy, Testimonial Evidence, and Narratives of Nation in Ghana's Postcolonial Democracy," *International Journal of African Historical Studies* 50, no. 2 (2017): 225–49.

43 PRAAD-Accra, ADM 5/3/143, J. B. Danquah to Kwame Nkrumah, Nsawam, [May 1964], in *Dr. J. B. Danquah: Detention and Death in Nsawam Prison: Extracts from Evidence of Witnesses at the Commission of Enquiry into Ghana Prisons* (Accra-Tema: Ministry of Information, 1967), 116, 117.

44 "One Party System Is the Only Solution to Progress," *Evening News,* January 10, 1964. More broadly, see Ahlman, *Living with Nkrumahism,* 153–57, 176–203.

45 Geoffrey Bing, *Reap the Whirlwind: An Account of Kwame Nkrumah's Ghana from 1950 to 1966* (London: MacGibbon & Kee, 1968), 246.

46 Dennis Austin, *Politics in Ghana, 1946–1960* (London: Oxford University Press, 1964), 414–15.

47 PRAAD-Sunyani, Brong Ahafo Regional Archives 1/1/20, [R. O. Amoako-Atta], February 1, 1964.

48 Ahlman, *Living with Nkrumahism,* 176–96.

Chapter 6: Exile and an Era of Reinvention

1 Jeffrey S. Ahlman, *Living with Nkrumahism: Nation, State, and Pan-Africanism in Ghana* (Athens: Ohio University Press, 2017), 204–6.

2 Gamal Nkrumah, "Fathia Nkrumah: Farewell to All That," *Al-Ahram Weekly On-line*, September 14–20, 2000, https://web.archive.org/web/20180114071705/http://weekly.ahram.org.eg/archive/2000/499/profile.htm.

3 Nkrumah, "Fathia Nkrumah." Published nearly simultaneously as Gamal Nkrumah's account, Nkrumah's literary executor June Milne offers a nearly identical account of the family's reaction to the coup in Milne, *Kwame Nkrumah: A Biography* (London: Panaf, 2000), 179–80.

4 Kwame Nkrumah, Statement to the Press, [ca. February 24, 1966], reproduced in Kwame Nkrumah, *Dark Days in Ghana* (New York: International Publishers, 1972), 10.

5 Nkrumah, *Dark Days in Ghana*, 11.

6 Nkrumah, 14–20; Milne, *Kwame Nkrumah: A Biography,* 187–88; Doreatha Drummond Mbalia, *Kwame Nkrumah: The June Milne Interview* (self-pub., 2019), 20.

7 Julie Medlock to Kwame Nkrumah, Cairo, May 4, 1966, reproduced in *Kwame Nkrumah: The Conakry Years: His Life and Letters,* ed. June Milne (London: Panaf, 1990), 41–42.

8 Moussa Conde (pseudonym) to Kwame Nkrumah, Lagos, July 21, 1966, in Milne, *Kwame Nkrumah: The Conakry Years,* 54–55.

9 Kwame Nkrumah to June Milne, July 8, 1966, in Milne, *Kwame Nkrumah: The Conakry Years,* 53.

10 Kwame Nkrumah, broadcast on Radio Guinea, "Voice of the Revolution," March 20, 1966, in Kwame Nkrumah, *Voice from Conakry* (London: Panaf, 1967), 10–11, quote on 10.

11 This is a theme throughout many, if not most, of Nkrumah's Radio Guinea addresses; Nkrumah, *Voice from Conakry.*

12 Ama Biney, "The Development of Kwame Nkrumah's Political Thought in Exile, 1966–1972," *Journal of African History* 50, no. 1 (2009): 90–99.

13 Harold Macmillan, "Address by Harold Macmillan to Members of Both Houses of the Parliament of the Union of South Africa, Cape Town, 3 February 1960," in Harold Macmillan, *Pointing the Way, 1959–1961* (New York: Harper & Row, 1972), 473–82.

14 Patrick Chabal, "National Liberation in Portuguese Guinea, 1956–1974," *African Affairs* 80, no. 318 (1981): 92.

15 Mabel Dove, "The Massacre of Innocent Africans," *Evening News,* June 2, 1961.

16 "Plight of Angolan Refugees: Babies Perish in Mothers' Arms," *Ghanaian Times,* June 24, 1961.

17 Alex Quaison-Sackey, quoted in "Ghana Accuses Portugal of Genocide in Angola," *Ghana Today,* February 14, 1962.

18 Kate Skinner, "West Africa's First Coup: Neo-colonial and Pan-African Projects in Togo's 'Shadow Archives,'" *African Studies Review* 63, no. 2 (2020): 375–98, esp. 384–85.

19 Kwame Nkrumah, *Africa Must Unite* (London: Panaf, 1963), 174.

20 Kwame Nkrumah, *What I Mean by Positive Action* (Accra: Convention People's Party, [1949]), 2–4.

21 Jeffrey S. Ahlman, "The Algerian Question in Nkrumah's Ghana, 1958–1960: Debating 'Violence' and 'Nonviolence' in African Decolonization," *Africa Today* 57, no. 2 (2010): 73–74. See also chapter 4 of this book.

22 Ibrahim Omar [Frantz Fanon], quoted in "Africa Tired of Foreign Domination," *Evening News,* December 10, 1958.

23 Frantz Fanon, *The Wretched of the Earth,* trans. Richard Philcox (New York: Grove Press, 1963); originally published as *Les damnés de la terre* (1961).

24 Kwame Nkrumah to June Milne, August 21, 1967, in Milne, *Kwame Nkrumah: The Conakry Years,* 174.

25 Ahlman, "The Algerian Question in Nkrumah's Ghana," 78–81; Ahlman, *Living with Nkrumahism,* 174.

26 Kwame Nkrumah to June Milne, April 30, 1966, in Milne, *Kwame Nkrumah: The Conakry Years,* 41.

27 Kwame Nkrumah to June Milne, May 18, 1966, in Milne, *Kwame Nkrumah: The Conakry Years,* 44.

28 Kwame Nkrumah to June Milne, April 8, 1969, in Milne, *Kwame Nkrumah: The Conakry Years,* 302.

29 Kwame Nkrumah, *Handbook of Revolutionary Warfare: A Guide to the Armed Phase of the African Revolution* (London: Panaf, 1968). Nkrumah put the finishing touches on *The Challenge of the Congo* while in exile in Conakry, but the bulk of the book was written while in Ghana.

30 Aide Memoire, Ambassador of Ghana to the United States to Secretary of State, Washington, DC, November 18, 1965, attached to Benjamin H. Read to Secretary of State, Washington, DC, November 27, 1965, in Lyndon Baines Johnson National Security Files, Africa: National Security Files, 1963–1969, reel 9.

31 Kwame Nkrumah, *Neo-colonialism: The Last Stage of Imperialism* (London: Thomas Nelson, 1965).

32 Nkrumah, *Handbook of Revolutionary Warfare,* 1 (emphasis in original).

33 Nkrumah, 5–8.

34 Kwame Nkrumah, *Class Struggle in Africa* (London: Panaf, 1970), 10–12, quotes on 10, 12.

35 Nkrumah, *Handbook of Revolutionary Warfare,* 15.

36 Kwame Nkrumah to June Milne, July 8, 1966, in Milne, *Kwame Nkrumah: The Conakry Years,* 53.

37 Fanon, *The Wretched of the Earth,* 23.

38 Nkrumah, *Handbook of Revolutionary Warfare,* 76–78; Nkrumah, *Class Struggle in Africa,* 75–79.

39 Fanon, *The Wretched of the Earth,* 66, 73–75.

40 Nkrumah, *Handbook of Revolutionary Warfare,* 80–88; Nkrumah, *Class Struggle in Africa,* 64–74.

41 Nkrumah, *Handbook of Revolutionary Warfare,* 88–95.

42 Nkrumah, 68–69, 96–97.

43 Nkrumah, 106–7.

44 Nkrumah, 108–22.

45 David Rooney, *Kwame Nkrumah: The Political Kingdom in the Third World* (New York: St. Martin's Press, 1988), 255–56, quote on 256.

Chapter 7: Remembering Nkrumah

1 June Milne, *Kwame Nkrumah: A Biography* (London: Panaf, 2000), 245–48, 253–57, quotes on 256, 257.

2 Milne, *Kwame Nkrumah: A Biography,* 258–62.

3 "Dr. Nkrumah Dies after Six Years in Exile," *Times of London,* April 28, 1972; "The Continuing Cult of Kwame Nkrumah," *Times of London,* April 28, 1972; Alden Whitman, "Nkrumah, 62, Dead; Ghana's Ex-Leader," *New York Times,* April 28, 1972; "Dr. Nkrumah Dies in Exile," *Times of India,* April 28, 1972.

4 Louise K. Hines, "I Knew Nkrumah," *Baltimore Afro-American,* May 6, 1972.

5 Ethel Payne, "Nkrumah: A Remembrance," *Chicago Defender,* May 6, 1972.

6 Milne, *Kwame Nkrumah: A Biography,* 258.

7 "Kwame Nkrumah is Dead," *Ghanaian Times,* April 28, 1972. See also "The Man, Nkrumah," *Ghanaian Times,* April 28, 1972.

8 Stokely Carmichael with Ekwueme Michael Thelwell, *Ready for Revolution: The Life and Struggles of Stokely Carmichael (Kwame Ture)* (New York: Scribner, 2003), 694–95.

9 Carmichael, *Ready for Revolution,* 694–95.

10 Amilcar Cabral, speech given at the symposium organized by the Democratic Party of Guinea, at the People's Palace in Conakry, on the occasion of the day dedicated to Kwame Nkrumah, May 13, 1972, reproduced in Amilcar Cabral, *Unity and Struggle: Speeches and Writings,* ed. Partido Africano da Independência da Guiné e Cabo Verde, trans. Michael Wolfers (New York: Monthly Review Press, 1979), 117.

11 Sékou Touré, quoted in Milne, *Kwame Nkrumah: A Biography,* 264.

12 Erica Powell, *Private Secretary (Female)/Gold Coast* (New York: St. Martin's Press, 1984), 220.

13 Samia Yaba Nkrumah, interview with Jacob U. Gordon, June 2, 2013, reproduced in Jacob U. Gordon, *Revisiting Kwame Nkrumah: Pathways for the Future* (Trenton, NJ: Africa World Press, 2017), 88.

14 Gamal Nkrumah, quoted in Carmichael, *Ready for Revolution,* 695.

15 "Nkrumah's Burial in Ghana Unsure," *New York Times,* May 7, 1972.

16 "Kwame to Be Buried at Nkroful," *Ghanaian Times,* May 1, 1972.

17 "Make Nkroful a Tourist Centre: Businessman Urges Govt," *Ghanaian Times,* May 8, 1972.

18 "Let There Be Peace," *Ghanaian Times,* May 15, 1972.

19 "Kwame Not Buried in Guinea," *Ghanaian Times,* May 16, 1972.

20 See, for instance, *Evening News,* October 14, 1961, quoted in David E. Apter, "Ghana," in *Political Parties and National Integration in Tropical Africa,* ed. James S. Coleman and Carl G. Rosberg Jr. (Berkeley: University of California Press, 1964), 304–5; and "Nkrumah Deserves the Name Messiah—Ako Adjei," *Evening News,* January 9, 1962. See also chapter 5 of this book.

21 Charles Andoh, "Nkrumah Never Dies," *Daily Graphic,* March 5, 2019, https://www.graphic.com.gh/features /features/ghananews-nkrumah-never-dies.html.

22 Andoh, "Nkrumah Never Dies."

23 Kwadwo Afari, "Nkrumah Never Dies, Unfortunately," *Daily Statesman,* March 7, 2019, http://thedailystatesman .com/index.php/news/item/7275-nkrumah-never-dies -unfortunately. The article was also reprinted in the *Ghanaian Chronicle* on March 12, 2019, with slight changes: http://thechronicle.com.gh/index.php/2019/03/12 /nkrumah-never-dies-unfortunately.

Bibliography

Archives

Ghana

George Padmore Research Library on African Affairs, Accra
Public Records and Archives Administration
    Department–Accra
Public Records and Archives Administration
    Department–Sunyani

United States

University of Massachusetts Amherst, Special Collections
    and University Archives
Yale University, Beinecke Rare Book and Manuscript Library
Yale University Library, Manuscripts and Archives

Microfilm Collections

Lyndon Baines Johnson National Security Files, Africa: National Security Files, 1963–1969 (Frederick, MD: University Publications of America, 1987)

Newspapers, Magazines, and Other Periodicals

African Morning Post (Accra)
Al-Ahram Weekly On-line (Cairo)
Ashanti Pioneer (Kumasi)
Baltimore Afro-American (Baltimore)

BBC News (London)
BBC World Service (London)
Chicago Defender (Chicago)
Daily Graphic (Accra)
Daily Statesman (Accra)
Evening News (Accra)
Ghana Today (Accra)
Ghanaian Chronicle (Accra)
Ghanaian Times (Accra)
Gold Coast Leader (Cape Coast)
New African (London)
New York Times (New York)
Spark (Accra)
Times of India (Bombay [Mumbai])
Times of London (London)
West African Pilot (Lagos)
West African Review (London)

Government Reports and Documents

All-African People's Conference. *Speeches by the Prime Minister of Ghana at the Opening and Closing Sessions on December 8th and 13th, 1958.* Accra: Community Centre, 1958.

Colonial Office. *Report of the Commission of Enquiry into Disturbances in the Gold Coast, 1948.* London: His Majesty's Stationery Office, 1948.

Colony of the Gold Coast. *Report on the Census for the Year 1901.* London: Waterlow and Sons, 1902.

Ghana, Republic of, National Assembly. *Parliamentary Debates: Official Report: First Series.* Accra: State Publishing Company, 1957–1966.

Government of the Gold Coast. *Blue Book, 1850.* London: Her Majesty's Stationery Office, 1850.

———. *Blue Book, 1899.* London: Her Majesty's Stationery Office, 1899.

Government of the Gold Coast, Legislative Assembly. *Legislative Assembly Debates: Official Report.* Accra: Government Printing Office, 1951–1956.

Published Books and Articles

Adi, Hakim. *Pan-Africanism and Communism: The Communist International, Africa and the Diaspora, 1919–1939.* Trenton, NJ: Africa World Press, 2013.

———. *West Africans in Britain 1900–1960: Nationalism, Pan-Africanism and Communism.* London: Lawrence & Wishart, 1998.

Aggrey, J. E. K. "The Prince of Wales College: A 'Wireless' Talk from London." *Southern Workman* 55, no. 1 (January 1926): 39–42.

Ahlman, Jeffrey S. "Africa's Kitchen Debate: Ghanaian Domestic Space in the Age of Cold War." In *Gender, Sexuality, and the Cold War: A Global Perspective,* edited by Philip E. Muehlenbeck, 157–77. Nashville, TN: Vanderbilt University Press, 2017.

———. "The Algerian Question in Nkrumah's Ghana, 1958–1960: Debating 'Violence' and 'Nonviolence' in African Decolonization." *Africa Today* 57, no. 2 (2010): 67–84.

———. *Living with Nkrumahism: Nation, State, and Pan-Africanism in Ghana.* Athens: Ohio University Press, 2017.

———. "Managing the Pan-African Workplace: Discipline, Ideology, and the Cultural Politics of the Ghanaian Bureau of African Affairs, 1959–1966." *Ghana Studies,* nos. 15/16 (2012–13): 337–71.

———. "A New Type of Citizen: Youth, Gender, and Generation in the Ghanaian Builders Brigade." *Journal of African History* 53, no. 1 (2012): 87–105.

———. "'The Strange Case of Major Awhaitey': Conspiracy, Testimonial Evidence, and Narratives of Nation in Ghana's Postcolonial Democracy." *International Journal of African Historical Studies* 50, no. 2 (2017): 225–49.

Allman, Jean Marie. *The Quills of the Porcupine: Asante Nationalism in an Emergent Ghana.* Madison: University of Wisconsin Press, 1993.

Allman, Jean, and Victoria Tashjian. *"I Will Not Eat Stone": A Women's History of Colonial Asante.* Portsmouth, NH: Heinemann, 2000.

Angelou, Maya. *All God's Children Need Traveling Shoes*. New York: Vintage, 1991.

Appiah, Joseph. *Joe Appiah: The Autobiography of an African Patriot*. Accra: Asempa, 1990.

Apter, David E. "Ghana." In *Political Parties and National Integration in Tropical Africa*, edited by James S. Coleman and Carl G. Rosberg Jr., 259–315. Berkeley: University of California Press, 1964.

Arhin, Kwame. *A View of Kwame Nkrumah, 1909–1972: An Interpretation*. Accra: Sedco, 1990.

Asante, S. K. B. *Pan-African Protest: West Africa and the Italo-Ethiopian Crisis, 1934–1941*. London: Longman, 1977.

Austin, Dennis. *Politics in Ghana, 1946–1960*. London: Oxford University Press, 1964.

———. "The Working Committee of the United Gold Coast Convention." *Journal of African History* 2, no. 2 (1961): 273–97.

Austin, Gareth. *Labour, Land, and Capital in Ghana: From Slavery to Free Labour in Asante, 1807–1956*. Rochester, NY: University of Rochester Press, 2005.

Awooner-Renner, Bankole. *West African Soviet Union*. London: WANS Press, 1946.

Azikiwe, Nnamdi. *My Odyssey: An Autobiography*. London: C. Hurst, 1970.

———. *Zik: A Selection from the Speeches of Nnamdi Azikiwe*. Cambridge: Cambridge University Press, 1961.

Banner-Haley, Charles Pete T. *To Do Good and To Do Well: Middle-Class Blacks and the Depression, Philadelphia, 1929–1941*. New York: Garland, 1993.

Barbot, Jean. *Barbot on Guinea: The Writings of Jean Barbot on West Africa, 1678–1712*. Edited by P. E. H. Hair, Adam Jones, and Robin Law. 2 vols. London: Hakluyt Society, 1992.

Biney, Ama. "The Development of Kwame Nkrumah's Political Thought in Exile, 1966–1972." *Journal of African History* 50, no. 1 (2009): 81–100.

———. *The Political and Social Thought of Kwame Nkrumah*. New York: Palgrave Macmillan, 2011.

Bing, Geoffrey. *Reap the Whirlwind: An Account of Kwame Nkrumah's Ghana from 1950 to 1966*. London: MacGibbon & Kee, 1968.

Bloom, Peter J., Stephan F. Miescher, and Takyiwaa Manuh, eds. *Modernization as Spectacle in Africa.* Bloomington: Indiana University Press, 2014.

Bond, Horace Mann. *Education for Freedom: A History of Lincoln University, Pennsylvania.* Lincoln University, PA: Lincoln University, 1976.

Brinkley, Douglas, and David R. Facey-Crowther, eds. *The Atlantic Charter.* New York: St. Martin's Press, 1994.

Buxton, Thomas Fowell. *The African Slave Trade and Its Remedy.* London: John Murray, 1840.

Cabral, Amilcar. *Unity and Struggle: Speeches and Writings.* Edited by Partido Africano da Independência da Guiné e Cabo Verde. Translated by Michael Wolfers. New York: Monthly Review Press, 1979.

Carmichael, Stokely, with Ekwueme Michael Thelwell. *Ready for Revolution: The Life and Struggles of Stokely Carmichael (Kwame Ture).* New York: Scribner, 2003.

Chabal, Patrick. "National Liberation in Portuguese Guinea, 1956–1974." *African Affairs* 80, no. 318 (1981): 75–99.

Coe, Cati. "Educating an African Leadership: Achimota and the Teaching of African Culture in the Gold Coast." *Africa Today* 49, no. 3 (2002): 22–44.

Coleman, James C., and Carl Rosberg Jr., eds. *Political Parties and National Integration in Tropical Africa.* Berkeley: University of California Press, 1964.

Coode, Thomas H., and John F. Bauman. *People, Poverty, and Politics: Pennsylvanians during the Great Depression.* Lewisburg, PA: Bucknell University Press, 1981.

Cronon, E. David. *Black Moses: The Story of Marcus Garvey and the Universal Negro Improvement Association.* 2nd ed. Madison: University of Wisconsin Press, 1969.

Danquah, Joseph Boakye. *Historic Speeches and Writings on Ghana.* Compiled by H. K. Akyeampong. Accra: George Boakie, 1970.

Du Bois, W. E. B. *The Philadelphia Negro: A Social Study.* Philadelphia: Publications of the University of Pennsylvania, 1899.

Edwards, Brent Hayes. *The Practice of Diaspora: Literature, Translation, and the Rise of Black Internationalism.* Cambridge: Harvard University Press, 2003.

Ewing, Adam. *The Age of Garvey: How a Jamaican Activist Created a Mass Movement and Changed Global Black Politics*. Princeton, NJ: Princeton University Press, 2014.

Fanon, Frantz. *The Wretched of the Earth*. Translated by Richard Philcox. New York: Grove Press, 1963. Originally published as *Les damnés de la terre* (1961).

Garvey, Marcus. *The Philosophy and Opinions of Marcus Garvey*. 2 vols. Edited by Amy Jacques-Garvey. New York: Universal Publishing, 1923–25.

George, Betty Stein. *Education in Ghana*. Washington, DC: Government Printing Office, 1976.

Gerzina, Gretchen. *Black London: Life before Emancipation*. New Brunswick, NJ: Rutgers University Press, 1995.

Getachew, Adom. *Worldmaking after Empire: The Rise and Fall of Self-Determination*. Princeton, NJ: Princeton University Press, 2019.

Gordon, Jacob U. *Revisiting Kwame Nkrumah: Pathways for the Future*. Trenton, NJ: Africa World Press, 2017.

Graham, C. K. *The History of Education in Ghana: From the Earliest Times to the Declaration of Independence*. London: Frank Cass, 1971.

Grant, Colin. *Negro with a Hat: The Rise and Fall of Marcus Garvey*. Oxford: Oxford University Press, 2008.

Grilli, Matteo. *Nkrumaism and African Nationalism: Ghana's Pan-African Foreign Policy in the Age of Decolonization*. New York: Palgrave Macmillan, 2018.

Hailey, William Malcolm. *An African Survey: A Study of Problems Arising in Africa South of the Sahara*. London: Oxford University Press, 1938.

Harsch, Ernest. *Thomas Sankara: An African Revolutionary*. Athens: Ohio University Press, 2014.

Higgins, Rosalyn. *United Nations Peacekeeping, 1946–1967: Documents and Commentary*, vol. 3, *Africa*. Oxford: Oxford University Press, 1980.

Hill, Polly. *The Gold Coast Cocoa Farmer: A Preliminary Survey*. London: Oxford University Press, 1956.

Hill, Robert A., ed. *The Marcus Garvey and Universal Negro Improvement Association Papers*, vol. 2, *27 August 1919–*

31 August 1920. Berkeley: University of California Press, 1983.

———. *The Marcus Garvey and Universal Negro Improvement Association Papers,* vol. 10, *Africa for the Africans, 1923–1945.* Berkeley: University of California Press, 2006.

Holden, Philip. *Autobiography and Decolonization: Modernity, Masculinity, and the Nation-State.* Madison: University of Wisconsin Press, 2008.

Ibhawoh, Bonny. "Second World War Propaganda, Imperial Idealism, and Anti-colonial Nationalism in British West Africa." *Nordic Journal of African Studies* 16, no. 2 (2007): 221–43.

Jackson, Sir Robert. "The Volta River Project." *Progress: Unilever Quarterly* 50, no. 282 (1964): 2–17.

James, C. L. R. *A History of Pan-African Revolt.* Chicago: Charles H. Kerr, 1995. Originally published as *A History of Negro Revolt* (1938).

James, Leslie. *George Padmore and Decolonization from Below: Pan-Africanism, the Cold War, and the End of Empire.* New York: Palgrave Macmillan, 2015.

Jopp, Keith. *Tema: Ghana's New Town and Harbour.* Accra: Ministry of Information and Broadcasting, 1961.

Kelley, Robin D. G. *Race Rebels: Culture, Politics, and the Black Working Class.* New York: Free Press, 1996.

Killingray, David. "Military and Labour Recruitment in the Gold Coast during the Second World War." *Journal of African History* 23, no. 1 (1982): 83–95.

———. "Soldiers, Ex-servicemen, and Politics in the Gold Coast, 1939–50." *Journal of Modern African Studies* 21, no. 3 (1983): 523–34.

Kimble, David. *A Political History of Ghana: The Rise of Gold Coast Nationalism, 1850–1928.* Oxford: Clarendon, 1963.

Lambert, Keri Grace. "Elastic Allegiances: Rubber, Development, and the Production of Sovereignties in Ghana, 1880–2017." PhD diss., Yale University, 2019.

———. "'In the Nature of a Crusade': Wartime Extraction and the Seeds of Industrialization in the Gold Coast." *Journal of West African History* 6, no. 1 (2020): 63–90.

———. "'It's All Work and Happiness on the Farms': Agricultural Development between the Blocs in Nkrumah's Ghana." *Journal of African History* 60, no. 1 (2019): 25–44.

Langley, J. Ayodele. *Pan-Africanism and Nationalism in West Africa, 1900–1945: A Study in Ideology and Social Classes.* Oxford: Clarendon, 1973.

Lenin, V. I. *Imperialism: The Highest Stage of Capitalism: A Popular Outline.* Revised translation. Moscow: Cooperative Publishing Society of Foreign Workers in the USSR, 1934. Originally published 1917.

Lindberg, Staffan I. *Democracy and Elections in Africa.* Baltimore: Johns Hopkins University Press, 2006.

Macmillan, Harold. *Pointing the Way, 1959–1961.* New York: Harper & Row, 1972.

Makonnen, [T.] Ras. *Pan-Africanism from Within.* Recorded and edited by Kenneth King. London: Oxford University Press, 1973.

Mazrui, Ali. "Nkrumah: The Leninist Czar." *Transition,* no. 26 (1966): 8–17.

Mbalia, Doreatha Drummond. *Kwame Nkrumah: The June Milne Interview.* Self-published, 2019.

McWilliam, H. O. A., and M. A. Kwamena-Poh. *The Development of Education in Ghana: An Outline.* London: Longman, 1975.

Metcalfe, G. E., ed. *Great Britain and Ghana: Documents of Ghana History, 1807–1957.* London: Thomas Nelson and Sons, 1964.

Miescher, Stephan F. "The Life Histories of Boakye Yiadom (Akasease Kofi of Abetifi, Kwawu): Exploring the Subjectivity and 'Voices' of a Teacher-Catechist in Colonial Ghana." In *African Words, African Voices: Critical Practices in Oral History,* edited by Luise White, Stephan F. Miescher, and David William Cohen, 162–93. Bloomington: Indiana University Press, 2001.

———. *Making Men in Ghana.* Bloomington: Indiana University Press, 2005.

———. "'Nkrumah's Baby': The Akosombo Dam and the Dream of Development in Ghana, 1952–1966." *Water History* 6, no. 4 (2014): 341–66.

———. "'No One Should Be Worse Off': The Akosombo Dam, Modernization, and the Experience of Resettlement in Ghana." In *Modernization as Spectacle in Africa*, edited by Peter J. Bloom, Takyiwaa Manuh, and Stephan F. Miescher, 184–204. Bloomington: Indiana University Press, 2014.

Mikell, Gwendolyn. *Cocoa and Chaos in Ghana*. Washington, DC: Howard University Press, 1992.

Milne, June. *Kwame Nkrumah: A Biography*. London: Panaf, 2000.

———, ed. *Kwame Nkrumah: The Conakry Years: His Life and Letters*. London: Panaf, 1990.

Muehlenbeck, Philip E. *Betting on the Africans: John F. Kennedy's Courting of African Nationalist Leaders*. Oxford: Oxford University Press, 2012.

———, ed. *Gender, Sexuality, and the Cold War: A Global Perspective*. Nashville, TN: Vanderbilt University Press, 2017.

Naison, Mark. *Communists in Harlem during the Depression*. Urbana: University of Illinois Press, 1983.

Nkrumah, Kwame. *Africa Must Unite*. London: Panaf, 1963.

———. *The Challenge of the Congo*. London: Thomas Nelson and Sons, 1967.

———. *Class Struggle in Africa*. London: Panaf, 1970.

———. *Dark Days in Ghana*. New York: International Publishers, 1972.

———. "Education and Nationalism in Africa." *Educational Outlook* 18, no. 1 (1943): 32–40. Published under the name Francis Nwia-Kofi Nkrumah.

———. *Ghana: The Autobiography of Kwame Nkrumah*. Edinburgh: Thomas Nelson and Sons, 1957.

———. *Handbook of Revolutionary Warfare: A Guide to the Armed Phase of the African Revolution*. London: Panaf, 1968.

———. *I Speak of Freedom: A Statement of African Ideology*. New York: Frederick A. Praeger, 1961.

———. *Neo-colonialism: The Last Stage of Imperialism*. London: Thomas Nelson, 1965.

——. *Revolutionary Path.* London: Panaf, 1973.

——. *Towards Colonial Freedom: Africa in the Struggle against World Imperialism.* London: Farleigh, 1947.

——. *Voice from Conakry.* London: Panaf, 1967.

——. *What I Mean by Positive Action.* Accra: Convention People's Party, [1949].

Osseo-Asare, Abena Dove. "Scientific Equity: Experiments in Laboratory Education in Ghana." *Isis: Journal of the History of Science Society* 104, no. 4 (2013): 713–41.

Padmore, George, ed. *Colonial and Coloured Unity: A Programme of Action: History of the Pan-African Congress.* London: Hammersmith Bookshop, 1963. First published in 1947 by the Pan-African Federation.

Powell, Erica. *Private Secretary (Female)/Gold Coast.* New York: St. Martin's Press, 1984.

Rathbone, Richard. *Ghana.* Vol. 1, pts. 1 and 2, of *British Documents on the End of Empire,* ser. B. London: Her Majesty's Stationery Office, 1992.

——. *Nkrumah and the Chiefs: The Politics of Chieftaincy in Ghana, 1951–1960.* Athens: Ohio University Press, 2000.

Rooney, David. *Kwame Nkrumah: The Political Kingdom in the Third World.* New York: St. Martin's Press, 1988.

Schmidt, Elizabeth. *Cold War and Decolonization in Guinea, 1946–1958.* Athens: Ohio University Press, 2007.

——. *Mobilizing the Masses: Gender, Ethnicity, and Class in the Nationalist Movement in Guinea, 1939–1958.* Portsmouth, NH: Heinemann, 2005.

Schneer, Jonathan. *London 1900: The Imperial Metropolis.* New Haven, CT: Yale University Press, 1999.

Scott, William R. *The Sons of Sheba's Race: African-Americans and the Italo-Ethiopian War, 1935–1941.* Bloomington: Indiana University Press, 1993.

Sherwood, Marika. *Kwame Nkrumah: The Years Abroad, 1935–1947.* Legon, Ghana: Freedom Publications, 1996.

Skinner, Kate. "West Africa's First Coup: Neo-colonial and Pan-African Projects in Togo's 'Shadow Archives.'" *African Studies Review* 63, no. 2 (2020): 375–98.

Terkel, Studs. *Hard Times: An Illustrated Oral History of the Great Depression.* New York: New Press, 1986.

Thompson, W. Scott. *Ghana's Foreign Policy, 1957–1966: Diplomacy, Ideology, and the New State.* Princeton, NJ: Princeton University Press, 1969.

Timothy, Bankole. *Kwame Nkrumah: His Rise to Power.* London: George Allen & Unwin, 1955.

White, Luise, Stephan F. Miescher, and David William Cohen, eds. *African Words, African Voices: Critical Practices in Oral History.* Bloomington: Indiana University Press, 2001.

Wraith, R. E. *Guggisberg.* London: Oxford University Press, 1967.

Wright, Richard. *Black Power: A Record of Reactions in a Land of Pathos.* New York: Harper and Brothers, 1954.

Zimmerman, Jonathan. "'Money, Materials, and Manpower': Ghanaian In-Service Teacher Education and the Political Economy of Failure, 1961–1971." *History of Education Quarterly* 51, no. 1 (2011): 1–27.

Index